ABC's

of A Strong Spiritual Life

Volume 1
A-M

Tiffany L. Secula

In Christian Love
Publishing

ISBN-13: 9781730768651

Edited by Maid to Edit
Dawn Weaver
Leitchfield, KY
www.maidtoedit.com

Published by
In Christian Love Publishing
Smiths Grove, KY

Dedicated to

My amazing husband, Nick,
who has always supported my dreams.

To all those ladies who have helped me with each of these lessons, I thank you. You have worked so hard helping me edit and make this book all it could be so we can all grow stronger in our lives to God.

To all my Christian sisters I have not yet had the opportunity to meet. May this study enrich your life and leave you longing to be with the Father every moment!

ABC's of A Strong Spiritual Life

ABC's of A Strong Spiritual Life

Introduction

In everything we start to learn or to do, we must start from the basics, from the beginning. That is the idea behind the lessons in the *ABC's of A Strong Spiritual Life*. These lessons are the product of over two years of study and teaching for our ladies' Bible class and have been enhanced to share with you.

As we dive right in, we must recognize something even more basic to this study than our ABC's: first, God is the One true and living God and Creator of this world, and second, the Bible is His holy and inspired Word.

> *"All Scripture is given by inspiration of God, and is profitable for doctrine, for reproof, for correction, for instruction in righteousness, that the man of God may be complete, thoroughly equipped for every good work." 2 Timothy 3:16-17*

(All Scriptures used in this study are drawn from the New King James version unless otherwise noted.)

I am going to assume that you would not be reading this book if you did not hold this belief. I admire that you are here, ready, and

eager to study God's Word and to grow in your spiritual life. God has given His words to us as our instructions for living and interacting with others and, ultimately, as our preparation for dying and leaving this material world for the greater spiritual life with Him.

As the verse above states, His words are profitable not just for the doctrine of truth and for knowing who God is, but for every other aspect of our lives. They reprove and correct us when we steer off course. His Word instructs us in the life of righteousness God would have us live to be like His Son.

All of this is so we may be complete, whole, lacking nothing as we live. The more we study and gain from it, the more we will find ourselves "thoroughly equipped" for every good work. We will have everything we need to live for Him, to work for Him, and to teach others about Him. God has given us all we need to be pleasing to Him, to learn who He is and what He expects from our lives.

"Grace and peace be multiplied to you in the knowledge of God and of Jesus our Lord, as His divine power has given to us all things that pertain to life and godliness, through the knowledge of Him who called us by glory and virtue." 2 Peter 1:2-3

In a sense, the Bible lays out a map for our lives, to guide our steps and lead us to Him. God shows us His desire for a relationship with His children, and He even details what we can do to have that relationship with our Father.

The *ABC's of A Strong Spiritual Life* is designed to draw out some necessary elements of that spiritual journey with the use of biblical references, character analysis, biblical definitions, and modern examples. A life close to God takes effort as well as faith, and this book is designed to help you be more Christ-like as you travel life's often rocky road.

The Bible is, without question, the most important book for us to read and study. By no means is this book to be a substitute for the daily study of God's Word. The *ABC's of A Strong Spiritual Life* is merely an outline of some of the godly characteristics needed in life, drawn together to help simplify the process and offer ideas of how to apply what you have learned in Scripture to your life.

I sincerely hope you enjoy this study and that it draws you deeper into the Word of God. May we all grow together in a clearer view of what God requires for a life lived fully for Him.

In Christian Love,

Tiffany

Using This Book

Hello, my sweet sister. Thank you for beginning your journey to a stronger spiritual life in your relationship with the Father. This book is intended to guide you as you study God's word and learn from Him ways to focus and grow closer to Him every day.

The ABC's of a Strong Spiritual Life can be used as either a personal Bible study or as part of a group study. There are 13 lessons designed to fit within a typical yearly quarter, or it can be done at a slower pace to meet your individual needs.

Within each lesson, you will find the chapter's lesson text filled with scriptural examples and truths to teach and guide you into a stronger spiritual life. Each lesson is designed so those who are both new to scripture and those who have more experience in its pages can gain insight and be encouraged. At the end of each lesson, there is a Power Verse chosen for memorization. Memorizing the Power Verse, which not only ties into the lesson topic, it will help encourage you during your day when you cannot be sitting at the feet of the Lord.

Each lesson also includes workbook pages with a variety of fill in the blank and short answer questions to help you consider the lessons from the text. These worksheets encourage you to once again think of the scriptures used in the lessons and what they mean for you. These questions are designed to open your heart and mind and guide you into considering your own life and how that the individual lesson pertains to you.

At the end of each lesson, you will find daily prayer and journal starters. For each day of the week, there is a correlating verse for you

to read and consider as well as thoughts to draw even more from the main idea of the lesson text and a question to help you narrow your focus. You can use these to direct your prayers or to journal your thoughts and continue your study of God's word. Your response to these journal prompts can be recorded in a regular notebook of your choosing or the ABC's of a Spiritual Life Companion Journal.

To conclude each chapter, there is a Deeper Study section. If you want to dig a little deeper into what the scripture teaches concerning the chapter's main subject, these study questions and readings are available to give you a place to begin. Each lesson that is prepared for you here covers only a portion of what God's word offers on a subject. You are encouraged to continue seeking His truth always as there will always be more to learn.

My prayer for you, sister, is that this book can be a tool to guide you into deeper studies of God's word, so your focus may be more and more on the Father.

A....... Admit Your Weaknesses

"Have mercy on me, O LORD, for I am weak;
O LORD, heal me, for my bones are troubled." Psalm 6:2

As we begin our journey to grow, step by step, in our spiritual walk with God, we need to understand just how much we need Christ in our lives. We must realize how weak and helpless we are without Him. We must learn to draw on His strength, not only to become the best we can be but to live truly.

Paul's Example – Read 2 Cor. 12:1-10   v. 9-10

The apostle Paul is a powerful example for us as we learn to admit our weaknesses and draw upon the incredible strength of Christ our Lord. Paul was given the opportunity by God to see some remarkable visions of heaven. He was also hindered by a thorn in the flesh, "a messenger of Satan," the Bible tells us, to keep him from boasting. Paul pleaded with God three times for this thorn to be removed, yet God's response was firm.

"And He said to me, "My grace is sufficient for you, for My
strength is made perfect in weakness." 2 Cor. 12:9a

God's strength works perfectly w/ my weakness

Paul had to learn to accept his new limitations and live with them. He had to draw from the strength of God to keep going each day and to finish the work he was commanded to do. His response of

15

humility and dependence is one we should reflect on in our own lives—a response that recognized that weakness and how God could use it.

> *"Therefore, most gladly I will rather boast in my infirmities, that the power of Christ may rest upon me. Therefore, I take pleasure in infirmities, in reproaches, in needs, in persecutions, in distresses, for Christ's sake. For when I am weak, then I am strong." 2 Cor. 12:9b-10*

God used this thorn to prove to Paul that, despite his physical weaknesses, God's strength was all he needed. Paul had to learn to admit that it wasn't by his own power or abilities that he was able to do the things he set out to do; rather it was through his dependence on God, the giver of true power and strength. When we learn to lean on God and not think we can do it all ourselves, we will realize how strong we become. We must learn to trust in Him and not in our abilities.

David's Understanding

David understood where his abilities came, and his life demonstrated this fact many times. From killing bears or lions to defeating the giant (1 Samuel 17), he wrote the truth of his understanding in Psalm 27:1,

> *"The LORD is my light and my salvation; Whom shall I fear? The LORD is the strength of my life; Of whom shall I be afraid?"*

When we have God's strength to lean on, we don't have to fear the things of this world. We can trust that we are already victorious through Him. However, to fully turn to Him, we must admit we are weak and realize how much help we need. David expressed his need for the Lord's strength during his times of weakness.

> *"Have mercy on me, O LORD, for I am weak; O LORD, heal me, for my bones are troubled." Psalm 6:2*

16

When David felt weak down to his bones and felt that he had nothing left in him to continue fighting, he always turned to God. David is an example of walking completely focused on God and dependent on His plan for life.

No matter what situation David was facing, he sought God. We see it in his challenge to the giant,

> *"You come to me with a sword, with a spear, and with a javelin. But I come to you in the name of the Lord of hosts, the God of the armies of Israel, whom you have defied." 1 Sam. 17:45*

We see it further as he asks the Lord what decisions to make in battle, *"Therefore David inquired of the Lord saying, 'Shall I go and attack these Philistines?'"* (1 Samuel 23:2) For even more examples, look at 1 Samuel 22:10, 23:4, and 30:8. David leaned heavily upon God!

When David failed to seek God's strength, we witness his weaknesses. He succumbed to lust, covetousness, adultery, lying, deceit, and ultimately murder. David's life shows us that even the strongest person, a man after God's own heart, is weak in the flesh without God. He faltered and fell hard when He did not lean on the strength of God for support. It will be the same for us when we are not honest with ourselves and when we fail to lean on God's everlasting powerful arm.

Asking for help isn't something that comes easily to most of us. We grow up thinking about being independent and doing it on our own. It is hard to admit we need help, that there are times when we can't do it ourselves. There is good news though! We can learn to ask Him for help when we don't think we can go on!

Jesus walked with the chosen twelve for three years of His ministry. During this time, while teaching them who He was and what their purpose would be, He taught them to depend on God. They were instructed to change their way of thinking on how things had always been done and to look to a new way, God's way. He challenged them to walk away from what they had known and to begin to depend on God.

17

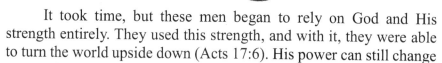

It took time, but these men began to rely on God and His strength entirely. They used this strength, and with it, they were able to turn the world upside down (Acts 17:6). His power can still change our world.

Isaiah also knew of the incredible strength God can offer to those who seek His help.

"They shall see the glory of the LORD, The excellency of our God. Strengthen the weak hands, And make firm the feeble knees."
Isaiah 35:2b-3

God created us as beings in need of strength and guidance from Him, our Creator. We were made to depend on Him. As we learn to do this in our own lives, we find the strength we never knew we had. We find our burdens easier to bear because we are not lifting them alone.

As we work in this life, we grow tired. As life wears on us with pain and trouble, we grow weary until we reach that point where we just can't go on. It is comforting to know that God never does! God does not grow faint. God does not need a break. We can always count on Him!

"Have you not known? Have you not heard? The everlasting God, the LORD, The Creator of the ends of the earth, Neither faints nor is weary. His understanding is unsearchable. He gives power to the weak, And to those who have no might He increases strength."
Isaiah 40:28-29

The Holy Spirit – Our Helper

There can come moments in our lives when we do realize we are weak, overwhelmed, and in need of God's help; yet we just do not know how to ask for it. We are hurting and confused and just cannot put the words together. We don't know where to begin. We are blessed that God knows and understands us more clearly than we know ourselves. He sent us a helper that intercedes for us during our most difficult times.

18

"Likewise the Spirit also helps in our weaknesses. For we do not know what we should pray for as we ought, but the Spirit Himself makes intercession for us with groanings which cannot be uttered."
Romans 8:26

As long as we are walking in the light of Christ, we will have the help we need. God will never give up on us nor forsake us.

The True Weakness

There is one weakness that, no matter how hard we try, we cannot overcome by ourselves, something everyone shares in. In Paul's letter to the Romans, he makes a statement that brings us to the heart of our need for Christ. Romans 3:23 reminds us that, *"all have sinned and fall short of the glory of God."* None but Jesus Himself have lived a perfect, sinless life. We have all made choices, chosen to sin, and separated ourselves from our Father in heaven.

"But your iniquities have separated you from your God, And your sins have hidden His face from you so that He will not hear."
Isaiah 59:2

Because of those sins, we lack the ability to make amends with our Lord; He can have no part with sin. The Bible teaches us that the wage for our sins is death (Romans 6:23). Christ knows and understands our weak, sinful state. He loved us regardless of it, and He came to earth and died so we may have life in Him.

"For when we were still without strength, in due time Christ died for the ungodly." Romans 5:6

Christ came and suffered on the cross to take away every weakness. He took away the weakness of sin and death and replaced it with power and life through Him. We have to admit the need for Him, though. We have to express that it is not of our own power, but His, and we must lean on Him in life and draw from that true power.

All strength in all things, in life and in death, comes from God. We should always seek this strength, just as Isaiah, knowing that,

19

"He gives power to the weak, and to those who have no might He increases strength." Isaiah 40:29

Power Verse

"I can do all things through Christ who strengthens me." Phil. 4:13

A....... Admit Your

Weaknesses

Worksheet

"Have mercy on me, O LORD, for I am weak;
O LORD, heal me, for my bones are troubled." Psalm 6:2

Paul's Example – 2 Cor. 12:1-10

Paul witnessed an amazing vision, but suffered with a <u>thorn</u>

in the <u>flesh</u> .

Through this, he learned that God's <u>grace</u> is sufficient.

vs. 10 "For when I am <u>weak</u>, then I am <u>strong</u> !"

When are times we feel at our weakest?

<u>fatigue - overwhelmed - lost - depth of sin - loss-</u>
<u>anger - frustration - stress - worry - discord - out</u>
<u>of fellowship w/God or His people - lonely - illness</u>

How can we draw from God's strength in these hard times?

<u>admit our weakness (sin), ask forgiveness, pray</u>
<u>talk to God, stillness, silence, focus on God</u>

David's Source of Strength

"The LORD is my light and my salvation; Whom shall I fear?
The LORD is the strength of my life; Of whom shall I be afraid?"
Psalm 27:1

From where did David draw his strength?

God, through prayer and supplication

"Have mercy on me, O LORD, for I am weak;
O LORD, heal me, for my bones are troubled." Psalm 6:2

What can we learn from David's example?

Even when David felt he could not go on, he always turned to God - who always gave him strength

Is it possible to turn to God when we face our own giants, just as David did, and trust He will help us through our struggles? How?

Yes, we know God is faithful and wants us to depend on Him in our times of trouble.

Can we <u>learn</u> to ask Him for help when we don't think we can go on and do it ourselves? How?

Yes, make it a point to ask for God's help even in the things we feel we do not need His help - becomes second nature

Asking for help is not something that comes easily to most of us. It is hard to admit we need help, that we can't do it ourselves. Isaiah knew,

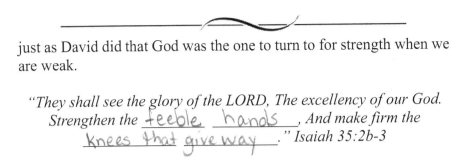

just as David did that God was the one to turn to for strength when we are weak.

"They shall see the glory of the LORD, The excellency of our God. Strengthen the feeble hands , And make firm the knees that give way ." Isaiah 35:2b-3

God Never Grows Weary!

"Have you not known? Have you not heard? The everlasting God, the LORD, The Creator of the ends of the earth, neither tired nor is weary . His understanding is unsearchable. He gives power to the weak, and to those who have no might He increases strength ." Isaiah 40:28-29

No matter how hard our troubles in life are, God never grows tired of helping us bear them!

The Holy Spirit – Our Helper

"Likewise the Spirit also helps in our weakness . For we do not know what we should pray for as we ought, but the Spirit Himself makes intercession for us with groanings which cannot be uttered." Romans 8:26

Sometimes we are so overwhelmed, we don't know even how to ask for help. How great is it to know we have someone on our side who can help us fill in the blanks? Does this thought bring you peace? Why?

Yes, it is reassuring to know that the Holy Spirit knows what we need and how to say it because we are weak and stumble in our life to find God

One Weakness We Can't Overcome Alone

"But your iniquities have separated you from your God; And your sins have hidden His face from you, So that He will not hear." Isaiah 59:2

The Bible teaches us that ___all___ have sinned. Romans 3:23

And that the wages of sin is ___death___. Romans 6:23
We can't erase our sins or do enough good to ever make them go away,
but......

*"For when we were still without ___power___, in due time
Christ died for the ungodly." Romans 5:6*

Christ has paid the price we could never pay! He has crossed that gap
that sin placed between God and us.

*"For there is one God and one Mediator ___between___ God and
men, the Man Christ Jesus," 1 Timothy 2:5*

In our weakest state, God grants us unimaginable, life-saving strength
through His Son!

*"He gives power to the weak, and to those who have no might He
increases ___strength___." Isaiah 40:29*

Daily Prayer and Journal Starters

Day 1 – John 3:16
God loves each of us so much that He gave the best gift Heaven could offer. How does this make you feel to know that you are so incredibly loved by the Creator of the whole world?

Day 2 – Romans 3:23
Since the entrance of sin into the world (Genesis 3), every person has proceeded to fall into sin personally. How has sin affected your life?

Day 3 – Isaiah 59:2
Sin has separated us from the God who loves us so deeply. Separation is hard. What does the reality of being apart from God mean to you?

Day 4 – Romans 5:8
Christ made the first move to reconnect with His separated creation. While we were without strength to do anything about our sins, while we were dead in them, He died to offer us salvation and forgiveness from those sins. This gift cost heaven everything yet is freely offered to each and every person.

Day 5 – 1 Timothy 2:5
The perfect sacrifice, who came and lived a sinless life here on earth and can fully relate to all our struggles, is now a mediator between sinful man and God the Father. Through Him, we have access once again to our Creator. Does that change your hope for life?

Day 6 – 1 Corinthians 15:21

Adam's sin in the garden opened the world to sin and death to all mankind. Christ's death and resurrection opened the world to redemption and salvation. There are only two paths for any of us to choose (Matthew 7:13-14). Which path do you choose?

Day 7 – Acts 2:37-38

An ultimate example of admitting weaknesses is found by the hearers of the first Gospel sermon on the day of Pentecost. Realizing that the weakness of their flesh, their sins, had crucified the very Son of God, they were driven to action. When we recognize our sins were part of that act, what does it motivate us to do? What does it drive us to change?

Deeper Study

The Psalms of David are a wonderful source for examples of a relationship with God. David, the man after God's own heart, showed us not only how to turn to God in our stronger moments, but particularly in our weaknesses. Read through the Psalms of David, noticing the attitude David has toward his own sin and the refuge offered by our God and Father.

B......Biblical Knowledge

"...but grow in the grace and knowledge of our Lord and Savior Jesus Christ. To Him be the glory both now and forever. Amen." 2 Peter 3:18

Once a person has admitted to needing the strength of God in his or her life, the next step is drawing upon that strength. As followers of God, everything we know, everything we do, and even everything we strive to be, we must learn from the Word of God. For growth personally, relationally, and ultimately spiritually, we need to grow in our Biblical knowledge.

Our purpose and power to live, our directions for living godly lives, and our examples to learn from are all found in the pages of the Bible. The good news for each of us is that the more we pour ourselves into studying the Word of God, the more knowledge we will gain regarding the way He desires for us to live. Every time we go to God's Word, we can learn something new. The more we dig into God's law, the stronger we will become.

God's Word is Our Weapon

As Christians, we are constantly bombarded by the injuries and temptations of this world. The Bible is our most powerful weapon for survival and the only way we have to

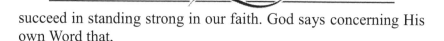

succeed in standing strong in our faith. God says concerning His own Word that,

"For the word of God is living and powerful, and sharper than any two-edged sword, piercing even to the division of soul and spirit, and of joints and marrow, and is a discerner of the thoughts and intents of the heart." Hebrews 4:12

Just as troops in an army need specific equipment to go into battle safely and effectively, so we as God's children need proper protection in our spiritual battle with sin. Our protection does not come from tanks and armor, but we from the Word of God.

"Stand therefore, having girded your waist with truth, having put on the breastplate of righteousness, and having shod your feet with the preparation of the gospel of peace; above all, taking the shield of faith with which you will be able to quench all the fiery darts of the wicked one. And take the helmet of salvation, and the sword of the Spirit, which is the word of God."
Ephesians 6:14-17

God gives us everything we need to keep us spiritually safe and on the road to heaven if we will only seek Him and trust that He is faithful to fulfill those needs. The more we study, the more we are able to use the abilities and weapons God has given us.

God's Word Is Our Tool

The Word of God is not some dusty old book on a shelf. It is alive and powerful. It is the most effective tool in a Christian's grasp. It speaks to us the very will of God. Not only does the Word of God teach us Who He is, but it also reveals who we are and our purpose for living. When we are active in the Word, it will live in us and change our hearts and minds to closely resemble that of God.

It is more than a tool to strengthen and defend us against temptation, it is our tool for examining our lives so we can weed

out those things which are against God and weigh our lives down with sin.

The Word of God gives us the standard by which we are to measure ourselves and keep ourselves to Jesus the Christ. In 2 Timothy 3:16-17, Paul teaches some of the uses for the inspired Scripture.

"All Scripture is given by inspiration of God, and is profitable for doctrine, for reproof, for correction, for instruction in righteousness, that the man of God may be complete, thoroughly equipped for every good work." 2 Timothy 3:16-17

Look closely at the words the apostle Paul used to describe the functions or Scripture.

Doctrine – It sets our beliefs about God and His plan for us, the plans He has carried out since the beginning of creation.

Reproof – God's Word points out the areas of our lives that are in the wrong, where we are at fault.

Correction – God's Word not only shows us the error of our ways but shows us how to correct our lives and bring those areas in line with Him.

Instruction in Righteousness – This takes correction a step farther and brings us toward a resemblance of God and His holiness. It instructs us in righteous living, not just living rightly.

These functions are for a purpose; the main goal is to make us complete. God desires each of His children to be whole, and we can only be that way in Him. We can be completely whole in a way this world will never be able to offer. When we become complete through God in our lives, then we will find that we are thoroughly equipped for every good work.

Approach God's Word with Purpose

These words given by God through the apostles are our "instructions" for living, but it is our responsibility to search it, know it, and apply it in our lives. God's Word must become a priority in our lives as we seek what it has to offer. Reading God's Word to change a life is more than just a casual glancing or even

short devotional moments, but it is approaching the Scripture with a purpose and intention.

> "You must give the Bible attention with intention, and it is intention that will necessitate attention... We must know what we are about." Henrietta Mears

When we approach God's Word, it must be done with the purpose of mind to hear what God is saying. The heart must have a purpose to look at it in such a way to seek change. We can see this in Scripture in the lives of some of God's people. As we look at verses such as Ezra 7:10, we can see Ezra's attitude toward approaching God's Word.

"For Ezra had prepared his heart to seek the Law of the LORD, and to do it, and to teach statutes and ordinances in Israel."

Ezra prepared his heart to be open to what God was teaching so that he could not only live it in his own life but also teach it to others. He had a purpose when approaching God's Word. He knew that for God's people to be what God desired, they needed to know His Word. We need that purpose to change our lives.

Sometimes, this idea of the in-depth study of God's Word can cause feelings of anxiety. The Bible consists of 66 books, thousands of pages, and can seem overwhelming to read and study. Study can and must start small, then grow as you learn and build a base of knowledge beneath you. A greater desire for knowledge and understanding of God's purpose in your life will grow within you as you continue to study His Word.

When overwhelming feelings arise, you may find yourself thinking: "Where do I begin?" "Do I need a study guide or commentary to understand this?" "What if I don't understand it?" The temptation when these feelings arise can be to turn to someone else to answer our Bible questions instead of investigating and studying them ourselves. However, we must be careful not to fall into the trap of he said/she said when it comes to Scripture. Even the most well-intentioned people can be wrong

from time to time because they are still imperfect humans. To combat this, we must be willing to seek out the meaning of God's Word for ourselves, never afraid to read and reread until we understand what God is telling us.

Each of us must strive to be like the early Christians recorded in the book of Acts,

> *"These were more fair-minded than those in Thessalonica, in*
> *that they received the word with all readiness, and searched the*
> *Scriptures daily to find out whether these things were so."*
> *Acts 17:11*

Other translations say they were more noble because they searched the Scripture daily, wanting to be sure that what they were being taught were the words of God and not just the words of men. We all must strive to be as diligent as the Bereans in our daily search for the truth of God.

The Need for Knowledge

In the Old Testament book of Hosea, the prophet pronounced that the people of God were being destroyed for lack of knowledge (Hosea 4:6). So many questions arise in our lives every day, and if we are without the knowledge of God, we will have no standard to guide us as we seek answers. Each choice we make can either draw us closer to Him and strengthen our walk of faith, or it can lead to our own destruction if we do not have the knowledge to make the godly choice.

Knowledge is powerful, and biblical knowledge is power from God Himself. The more we know of His Word, the more capable we will become. Solomon wrote in Proverbs 24:5, *"A wise man is strong, Yes, a man of knowledge increases strength."* Our strength to lead godly lives grows as we dig ever deeper into God's Word.

Just as the Christians in Acts 17, we must be a people who strengthen ourselves in the Word daily. There is another passage in the Old Testament which better visualizes this idea of daily focusing on God's Word. In Deuteronomy 6:4-9, Moses is still early in his recapping of the law for the children of Israel as they

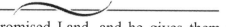

are about to enter the Promised Land, and he gives them this reminder.

"Hear, O Israel: The LORD our God, the LORD is one! You shall love the LORD your God with all your heart, with all your soul, and with all your strength. And these words which I command you today shall be in your heart. You shall teach them diligently to your children, and shall talk of them when you sit in your house, when you walk by the way, when you lie down, and when you rise up. You shall bind them as a sign on your hand, and they shall be as frontlets between your eyes. You shall write them on the doorposts of your house and on your gates."

The people of God were commanded to be diligent in the Word of God. They were to have it in their hearts, to focus on it, to teach it as they were in their house or walking outside when they lay down to rest or rose in the morning. God's Word was to be in front of their eyes at all times of the day, no matter where they were or what they were doing. Every aspect of their daily lives was to be centered on the very Word of God, and so should ours.

Diligence in God's Word

The commands given through Moses for daily focus on God's Word reached beyond the average citizen all the way to the king. In Deuteronomy 17:18-19, instructions are given for all future kings of Israel,

"Also it shall be, when he sits on the throne of his kingdom, that he shall write for himself a copy of this law in a book, from the one before the priests, the Levites. And it shall be with him, and he shall read it all the days of his life, that he may learn to fear the LORD his God and be careful to observe all the words of this law and these statutes."

The leaders of God's people were to be in the Word all the days of their lives, even writing their own copy of the law in order to focus upon it and know it deeply. As Christians, we are kings

and priests of God and should give the same diligence to His Word daily (1 Thess. 2:13; Rev. 1:6; 5:10).

Rightly Dividing the Word

In the New Testament, Paul wrote to Timothy telling him to study to show himself approved of God. When we are walking under God's authority, those around us will see the difference He has made in our lives.

> *"Be diligent to present yourself approved to God, a worker who does not need to be ashamed, rightly dividing the word of truth." 2 Timothy 2:15*

To rightly divide God's Word, we must take it as a whole work and believe it in its entirety. God's Word should never be believed on one part and rejected on another. We must read and study to discover what God says to us, not what we want to make His Word say to agree with our thoughts and desires.

As we approach Scripture, we must always look to His Word to find what He is saying. We need to guard against picking and choosing verses that seem to prove our own preconceived thoughts and ideas. Our hearts must be open to receive His truth, not our own version of it. God's Word must be taken as a whole to gain as much from it as possible so that our knowledge and faith can be expanded.

Bending Scripture into something it was not meant to be is not a new concept. Even in Peter's day, there were people who would twist the Scriptures to their own ideas. Either they couldn't understand what was said, or they didn't want to because it would interfere with a part of their lives they were not willing to give up. Peter explained this idea in 2 Peter 3:16,

> *"...as also in all his epistles, speaking in them of these things, in which are some things hard to understand, which untaught and unstable people twist to their own destruction, as they do also the rest of the Scriptures."*

We must be careful to never fall into that trap. God's Word cannot change to meet the changing world views. The world must change and come to know the unchanging Word of God. Just as Jesus is the same yesterday, today, and forever (Heb. 13:8), we can rest assured the same is true for His Word!

Since the days of Adam and Eve, mankind has sought the knowledge of God. Access to that knowledge is now easier than ever, and we have the freedom in this country to seek it as we wish. God will no longer overlook ignorance of His Word (Acts 17:30), but has given us access to it and calls all men to repentance through it.

Understanding our sin, and the wages of that sin can lead us to want to change. A healthy fear of the Lord and His power, says Solomon, leads to knowledge (Proverbs 2:1-7). Our God is the God of knowledge, and He wants to share it with us!

"For the LORD is the God of knowledge;
And by Him actions are weighed." 1 Samuel 2:3b

Solomon firmly understood this point. When given his choice of anything in the world that God could give to him, he chose knowledge and wisdom. He understood, probably better than anyone else, where to turn for knowledge (2 Chronicles 1:7-12). Because of this choice, God granted him that knowledge and much more as well. God wants us to make the same choice. In James 1:5, we are told if we lack wisdom, we need to ask it of God, Who gives "liberally and without reproach." As we seek His knowledge through His Word, He will bless us with that knowledge!

Power Verse

"Oh, how I love Your law! It is my meditation all the day. You, through Your commandments, make me wiser than my enemies; For they are ever with me."
Psalm 119:97-98

34

B....... Biblical Knowledge

Worksheet

"...but grow in the grace and knowledge of our Lord and Savior Jesus Christ. To Him be the glory both now and forever. Amen."
2 Peter 3:18

In what areas can Christians find the Word of God useful in their daily lives?

_____

_____

_____

_____

God's Word is Our Weapon
"For the word of God is _____ and _____, and sharper than any two-edged _____, piercing even to the division of soul and spirit, and of joints and marrow, and is a discerner of the thoughts and intents of the heart."
Hebrews 4:12

Consider Ephesians 6:14-17. Thinking about the Word of God as our protection from the world, in what ways can you use this armor in your personal life? In your relationships? Against your temptations, etc.?

God's Word is Our Tool

In 2 Timothy 3:16-17, Paul gives a list of functions for the inspired Scripture.

It is profitable for _____, _____, _____, _____ in _____.

To make us ... _____, Thoroughly Equipped for _____ _____ _____.

What good works can you do for God as you grow in the knowledge of His Word?

_____
_____
_____
_____

Approach God's Word with Purpose

"For Ezra had _____ his heart to seek the Law of the LORD, and to do it, and to teach statutes and ordinances in Israel." Ezra 7:10

In what ways can you prepare your heart to be open to receive the truth of God?

_____
_____
_____
_____

"These were more fair-minded than those in Thessalonica, in that they received the word with _____ _____, and _____ the Scriptures _____ to find out whether these things were so." Acts 17:11

The Need for Knowledge
"A wise man is strong, yes, a man of _____
increases strength." Proverbs 24:5

Thinking of the passage in Deut. 6:4-9, what are some steps you can take to focus on the Word of God throughout your day?

_____
_____
_____
_____

Diligence in God's Word
Just as the kings of Israel were commanded to be in the Word of God daily and to write their own copy of the law, consider writing Scripture for yourself. It not only helps you memorize passages to keep them in your heart, but it gives you a deeper understanding and appreciation for the message of God.

Rightly Dividing the Word
"Be diligent to present yourself approved to God, a worker who does not need to be ashamed, _____ _____ the word of _____." 2 Timothy 2:15

We must desire to know more about God and His will for our lives, to strive to be more like our Lord. He is the God of...

"For the LORD is the God of _____;
And by Him actions are weighed." 1 Samuel 2:3b

Daily Prayer and Journal Starters

Day 1 – Psalm 1:1-2
A blessed man (or woman) is one who meditates on the law, the Word of God, day and night. God's blessings are different from the world's. Think about the ways God blesses a life spent focused on Him and His Word. What blessings do you see in your life?

Day 2 – 1 Samuel 2:3b
The Lord is the God of knowledge, and He wants His people to be knowledgeable of Him and His Word. Our every action and deed will be weighed based on His Word (John 12:48). If we desire to be pleasing to the Lord, shouldn't we know how He wants us to live?

Day 3 – Proverbs 18:15
The heart that is concerned for the future seeks knowledge to allow for the best life to be lived. Proverbs 1:7 tells us that knowledge begins with the fear of the Lord. If we are concerned with not only our future life here on earth but our future eternal life, then we need the knowledge of God. How does God's wisdom differ from man's idea of knowledge? Where will the knowledge of man lead?

Day 4 – Joshua 1-8
As the people entered the new land, God instructed Joshua not to let the Book of the Law, God's Word, depart from his mouth. He was to be constantly in God's Word in order to lead God's people. Imagine if today's leaders were meditating on God's Word day and night. What differences would you see in the world?

Day 5 – Psalm 119:73

God can help lead us to understand when we are constantly in His Word. Praying for His guidance, just as David did, is a great place to start. Asking the Lord to help us to know Him and His Word leads to greater understanding. Consider James 1:5. In what areas of God's Word you would desire greater understanding?

Day 6 – John 17:17

God only speaks the truth. He cannot lie (Psalm 24:4, Titus 1:2). His Word is something we can have faith in. We do not have to worry about being led astray. Since His Word is truth, compare all the things the world tells us against the Word of God. Do they match? Which should be trusted? Which words will lead you on a path and direction of safety?

Day 7 – Psalm 119:105

This world is full of darkness. It is hard for us to see, but God's Word gives us light. As you struggle to find your way in the darkness, where can this light lead you? Are there dark areas of your life that His light can expose and help you correct?

Deeper Study

Read Psalm 119, particularly verse 72. Consider David's feelings towards the words of God. God's Word is a treasure more valuable than the riches of this world. In Matthew 6:19-21, Jesus spoke about laying up treasures in heaven. Consider your life. What treasures are you laying up for the future? Do you find treasure in God's Word? Find verses that remind you of the value of following God's law.

.... Notes ....

C.......Commitment to Christ

"Therefore, let those who suffer according to the will of God commit their souls to Him in doing good, as to a faithful Creator." 1Peter 4:19

To see anything through from beginning to end requires commitment. When life gets tough, when obstacles or temptations arise in anything we attempt to do, there must be a level of commitment in what we are reaching toward, or we will not succeed. Without commitment and dedication in life, we will falter. The Christian walk is no exception. To grow stronger in our spiritual lives, there must be a commitment to carry us through the temptations, persecutions, troubles, and bad days.

Most everyone knows and understands the word *commitment* when used in our everyday lives. It is the making of a promise or a pledge to get something done. We make a commitment to be somewhere at a specified time or to offer assistance on a project. We hold a commitment to our relationships or even to repay a loan at the bank.

We also understand the consequences when we choose to break those commitments. However, when it comes to our spiritual lives, the word *commitment* doesn't always seem to hold the same meaning.

The Merriam Webster dictionary defines *commitment* as "an act of committing to a charge or trust, an agreement or pledge to do something in the future, or the state or an instance of being obligated or emotionally impelled."

Being committed, obligated, emotionally impelled, and tied to a person or cause is to want to do for them, to make them a part of who we are, regardless of the personal cost. When we fully realize what Christ has done for our lives, and we desire to live for Him on His terms, we must make a commitment to Him.

He wants us to make a change that is full and complete and meant to last the rest of our lives. Christ wants <u>ALL</u> of our lives, not the leftovers. He wants to be our everything, our top priority in life, not something we set on the back burner to be called upon when it's convenient. The life He wants us to live requires that full commitment to Him!

Looking again at the passage in Deuteronomy 6, we see familiar words. Verse 5 contains the same words Jesus repeats when asked about the greatest command, as recorded in Matthew 22:36-40.

"You shall love the LORD your God with all your heart, with all your soul, and with all your strength." Deut. 6:5

We have to love God, but it is more than just having a love for God; it must be a love that commits us to God. This kind of love flows from every part of who we are.

- Our heart – our emotions and our thoughts – God gave us our emotions, and we need to use them to glorify Him; our thoughts and our minds should be focused on Him and His will always.
- Our soul – our spirit – our eternal soul, the image of God, the part that will spend eternity with Him must be committed to living like Him in this life.
- Our strength – our bodies – our physical selves and the work they do for Him should be to His glory.

Everything that we are must be in love with and be dedicated to our Lord; that is the kind of commitment God is

seeking from His children, the kind that makes every choice and decision based on the will of God and not the desires of self.

Commitment and Devotion of Ruth

The Bible is full of examples of lives showing this great commitment to God. A beautiful example of commitment and devotion can be seen in the life of Ruth. Ruth was a Moabite woman who married an Israelite who came to town with his family. Shortly after, however, her husband, her brother-in-law, and father-in-law all passed away.

Even after such devastating events in the lives of her and her mother-in-law, events that would knock most people off their feet, she shows her true character, her true level of commitment to family and to the God she learned of from her husband's family. Ruth demonstrated a commitment that was unshakable even in the midst of tragedy. Even when her sister-in-law departed and turned back to her old life, Ruth was steadfast in her commitment. Ruth's words of devotion to her mother-in-law are some of the sweetest words ever spoken.

"But Ruth said: 'Entreat me not to leave you, or to turn back from following after you; For wherever you go, I will go; And wherever you lodge, I will lodge; Your people shall be my people, And your God, my God. Where you die, I will die, and there will I be buried. The LORD do so to me, and more also, If anything but death parts you and me.'" Ruth 1:16-17

Naomi must have been a powerful example to Ruth to have led her to that kind of commitment. Her commitment to the Lord and to her family changed the course of their entire lives to the extent of placing this foreign woman in the genealogy of the Christ.

To be as spiritually strong as is needed to withstand the pressures and temptations of this world, we must have that kind of complete commitment to Christ. In 1 Peter 4:19, we are told directly that commitment is required.

"Therefore, let those who suffer according to the will of God commit their souls to Him in doing good, as to a faithful Creator."

Not only are we commanded to commit our souls to God, but the command continues to show that our actions in life must be part of that commitment. It is a full commitment to doing good in Him. A commitment that brings about active changed living.

Commitment Is Visible

As children of the Most High God, we must be committed to living His Way, by His commands. It should cause a change in our lives that is visible to those around us. The people we come into contact with should be able to see our lives and recognize that we are different from the world. We are told to *"let your light shine before men, that they may see your good works and glorify your Father in heaven."* (Matt. 5:16) A life committed to Christ will shine His light out into the world and draw others to Him.

Commitment Requires Sacrifice

As we are striving to live for Him and let our commitment be seen by those around us, we must stay vigilant that we place nothing in our lives above our relationship with Christ. As part of being committed to Him, we must always be willing to choose Him and His will above all else. Harder still, we must be willing to place His will above our own.

In Luke 14, we read of the great multitude that followed Jesus. He spoke to the crowd words that sound out of place from the God of love. He said to them,

"If anyone comes to me and does not hate his father and mother, wife and children, brother and sisters, yes, and even his own life also, he cannot be my disciple." vs. 26

No, Jesus who is love is not telling the world to hate, but stating in a most powerful way that He must be placed above all. Paul wrote in Galatians 2:20 about this powerful crucifying of self.

"I have been crucified with Christ; it is no longer I who live, but Christ lives in me; and the life which I now live in the flesh I live by faith in the Son of God, who loved me and gave Himself for me."

Paul and so many Christians after him realized that to be committed to Christ and wear His name, we must put away the desires of our own heart for His. His will must come before our own, His commands before our ideas or comforts.

The Rich Young Ruler

There is an example of someone who did not choose this path in the book of Matthew, chapter 19. There is an encounter between Jesus and a rich young ruler who comes to the Lord asking what he must do to inherit eternal life. He confesses that he has kept the commandments from his youth; yet when Jesus challenges him to place the commands of Jesus above his own life (in this case his wealth), he walks away filled with sorrow.

His example shows that true commitment requires so much more than just having knowledge of who Jesus is; it takes that change in our lives that this young man was not willing to make. This unnamed man knew who Jesus was, he knew the words that were taught concerning Him, and he fully knew the commandments of God; however, he was not willing to do what Jesus asked of him. When asked to give up his possessions and place Jesus first in his life, to the position of importance above all else, the young man went away sorrowful.

He loved his many possessions more than he loved Jesus. The true commitment did not reside within him. He was not willing to make the necessary changes in his life for Christ.

Other Lives of Great Commitment

There are so many other lives in Scripture in which we can read of their great commitment to the cause of the Lord. They show us their determination to stay with the Lord no matter what the world threw at them. We can learn something from each of

them about keeping our own lives committed to the cause of Christ.

Noah – A man who preached to an immoral world for 100 years while building an ark that no one else understood. We can only imagine what he and his family endured; we know how cruel people can be toward others. Yet, he pushed ever onward and saved his family, and guaranteed the continued existence of all the animals, because of his faithfulness.

Abraham – A man willing to leave the only land he knew for an unknown destination. When he was 75-years-old, he was promised by God that he would have a son, and Abraham waited for that son until he was 100-years-old. This same man was willing, fully trusting in God, to offer that son back to God; he understood that if God had promised a great nation through him, God was capable of raising that son from the ashes.

Moses – A man willing to give up a life of royalty and riches, being raised in the household of Pharaoh, to follow the will of God and join his persecuted Israelite family. Moses followed the commands of God to save his people, only to have them continually turn against him and grumble about their situation. He spent a lifetime leading a people who kept turning against him.

Joseph – A man who had grand visions of life for God, yet those around him tried to keep him from it. Not life in the pit, life as a slave, false accusations, imprisonment, abandonment, or rejection could break his commitment to God. He had a different spirit, a spirit that was focused on God!

Stephen – A Christian man whose life was so committed to teaching others about Jesus that he continued even unto death. His commitment led him to the title of the first martyr.

Of course, the greatest example of all is Jesus. 1 Peter 2:23 tells us,

"Who, when He was reviled, did not revile in return; when He suffered, He did not threaten, but <u>committed</u> Himself to Him who judges righteously."

Even when treated worse than we can ever imagine, He didn't fight back or threaten, but committed Himself to the righteous Judge.

Ways We Can Strengthen Our Commitment

As we go about our daily lives, there are some ways we can purposely strive to strengthen our commitment to our Lord and Savior.

Make Him a Priority! Just as you make family, career, or education a priority for your attention, put Him at the top of your list! When you focus on Him and His will as being important in your life, you will begin to strengthen your relationship with Him.

Spend More Time with God. Spending time in His Word and in prayer with the Father will keep Him on your mind and in your life. The more time you spend with anyone, the stronger your relationship with them grows, the same is true with God. This is exactly what He desires from us, a strong relationship with constant conversation.

Consider God During Your Day! Are your thoughts and actions during the day such as God would approve of? Would He be proud of you? Consider Him during your day as if He was standing beside you because He is! As you keep your thoughts focused on Him, you will find it easier and easier to do so!

Be Involved! When you involve yourself in the works and responsibilities of His church, you will find yourself more committed to Him and His family. As you are more committed to working for His will, you will find it harder to let it go. The more time you spend with the family of God, the harder it will be to

miss out on the important, spiritually strengthening aspects that come with being a part of His family.

Involve Others! When you are sharing God and your faith with others, you will find it encourages your faith as well. When you are excited about something in your life, others become excited as well. When you include your family and friends in something as important as worshiping and celebrating God together, you will strengthen each other's commitment to Him. You will have a support system to turn to in hard times and to keep you on the right path!

As we look back again at Deuteronomy 6, we can see these methods of commitment commanded to be followed in the lives of the Hebrew family.

"And these words which I command you today shall be in your heart. You shall teach them diligently to your children, and shall talk of them when you sit in your house, when you walk by the way, when you lie down, and when you rise up. You shall bind them as a sign on your hand, and they shall be as frontlets between your eyes. You shall write them on the doorposts of your house and on your gates." Deut. 6:6-9

We cannot do, or teach, or be from something we do not have. God desires we commit His Word to our hearts, close to us, kept special, treasured, near at all times so we can use it no matter what.

We can use His Word to teach our children and grandchildren; we can teach anyone we come into contact with— family, friends, neighbors, and co-workers! We are to tell others about the wonderful love of Christ!

God doesn't even specify that we take extra time out of our already busy lives to take care of this. When then are we to share our commitment to God with others? When our schedules are already so busy, when are we supposed to have the time to teach others?

The answer lies as we finish the passage. Look again in verse 7. God desires our thoughts and actions to show our

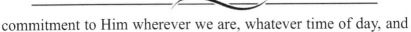

commitment to Him wherever we are, whatever time of day, and whatever we are doing. Every moment of every day is the perfect time to remember God and share something of Him with those around you!

This passage set the attitude that the Hebrews, the Jews, carried with them every day, even through the establishment of the church. They would keep the Word of God sewn into their clothing, tied to their wrists, any way possible to keep it close by. Do we have that same commitment in our lives to cling to God and His Word constantly?

We should live our lives so that God's Word is in every aspect of it!

Power Verse

"Only fear the Lord, and serve Him in truth with all your heart; for consider what great things He has done for you."
1 Samuel 12:24

C.......Commitment to Christ

Worksheet

"Therefore let those who suffer according to the will of God commit their souls to Him in doing good, as to a faithful Creator." 1Peter 4:19

What does commitment mean to you?

_____

_____

_____

_____

What things in your life are you committed to?

_____

_____

_____

_____

Christ wants the _____ of our lives, not the leftovers.

"You shall love the LORD your God with _____ your heart, with _____ your soul, and with _____ your strength."
Deut. 6:5

We have to love God with a love that commits us to Him, the kind of love that flows from every part of who we are.

50

- Our _____ – our emotions and our thoughts
- Our _____ – our spirit
- Our _____ – our bodies

Commitment and Devotion of Ruth

Ruth changed her whole life to follow Naomi, leaving her family, her friends, and her gods. Are there things in your life you would need to leave behind to be devoted to God?

_____
_____
_____
_____

Think about Ruth's words of commitment to Naomi.

"But Ruth said: "Entreat me _____ to leave you, or to turn back from following after you; For wherever you go, I will go; And wherever you lodge, I will lodge; Your people shall be my people, And _____ God, _____ God. Where you die, I will die, and there will I be buried. The LORD do so to me, and more also, If anything but death parts you and me."
Ruth 1:16-17

Think about your commitment to God. What would you be willing to commit to Him?

_____
_____
_____
_____

"Therefore, let those who suffer according to the will of God _____ their souls to Him in _____ _____, as to a faithful Creator." 1 Peter 4:19

What actions can you change in your life to show your growing commitment to God?

_____

Commitment Is Visible

"Let your light shine before men, that they may _____ your good works and glorify your Father in heaven" Matt. 5:16.

What does your light shine forth to show?

_____

_____

_____

_____

Commitment Requires Sacrifice

What is there in your life that may take the place of priority over God?

_____

_____

_____

_____

What changes can you picture in your life when you willingly commit to Him?

_____

_____

_____

_____

"I have been _____ with Christ; it is no longer ____ who live, but _____ lives in me; and the life which I now live in the flesh I live by faith in the Son of God, who loved me and gave Himself for me." Galatians 2:20

What are some things in your life that get placed before God?

_____

_____

_____

_____

The Rich Young Ruler
The rich young ruler in Luke 14 was unwilling to part with what he held dear in order to follow Jesus. How do you imagine his life would have changed if he had given up all to commit to the Lord?

_____

_____

_____

_____

Are you willing to make the necessary sacrifices for the One who sacrificed all for us?

Other Lives of Great Commitment
As you read of the lives of these great examples, what sticks out to you concerning their commitment to God?

Noah –

_____

_____

_____

Abraham –

_____

_____

_____

Moses –

_____

_____

_____

Joseph –

_____

Stephen –

Jesus –

"who, when He was reviled, did not revile in return; when He suffered, He did not threaten, but _____ Himself to Him who judges righteously;" 1 Peter 2:23

Think of your own life. Do you leave your troubles in the capable hands of God or do you seek worldly ways of addressing them?

How would your commitment have handled lives and moments like the examples above?

Ways We Can Strengthen Our Commitment
For each item, think of one thing you can change in your life to strengthen your commitment to Him.

Make Him a Priority!

Spend More Time with God.

_____

_____

_____

Consider God During Your Day!

_____

_____

_____

Be Involved!

_____

_____

_____

Involve Others

_____

_____

_____

We should live our lives so that God's Word is in every aspect of it!

Daily Prayer and Journal Starters

Day 1 – Joshua 22:5
As Joshua is speaking to the children of Israel, he points out the importance of staying in the Word of God. He says to take careful heed to do the commandments. Notice the other action words in that verse and think of what actions you can choose to stay in the Word of God?

Day 2 – 1 Chronicles 28:9
The great king David spoke some powerful words to his son and future king. Think of this verse, in which David instructs him to serve God with a loyal heart, and imagine he is saying it directly to you. How do you feel about this insight which tells us God knows our hearts?

Day 3 – Romans 1:21
The people in the first century, and many people since rejected worshipping God as Lord, even with knowledge of who He was. They had the head-knowledge, but no commitment to serve Him. If we lose or fail to have the commitment to serve God, how will that change our approach to life, especially when trouble arises?

Day 4 – 2 Peter 1:2-6
God has given us all things that pertain to life and godliness (vs. 3) and has asked that we give all diligence (vs. 5) to a life for Him. Think of the word *diligence* in relation to the qualities listed that we are told to add to our lives. Each of them requires a commitment, in and of themselves. How does your commitment to God grow as you diligently work to add these to your life?

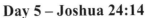

Day 5 – Joshua 24:14

Joshua's command for the children of Israel to put away the gods of their fathers reminds us to put away anything that stands between God and us. His instructions are to serve God in sincerity and truth. How can knowing the truth of God help to keep Him at the forefront of our thoughts and focus?

Day 6 – Romans 6:17-18

Every one of us sins; no one is perfect (Romans 3:23). When we obey God's commands from the heart, He saves us from the wages of those sins, which is death (Romans 6:23). Thinking of what Christ has done to redeem you from your sins, how does that impact the level of commitment you feel to serve Him?

Day 7 – Romans 12:1-2

To present ourselves as a living sacrifice takes true commitment to the cause of Christ. Commitment that changes us from the inside out, making us different from the world and more like Christ. It is our reasonable service for all He has done for us. Think about your commitment to Him. How can you use the examples of this lesson to deepen your commitment to Him?

Deeper Study

Read Genesis 29, 37, and 39-50, and consider all the obstacles that faced Joseph in his life. There are so many things that could have caused him to turn his back on God, yet he stayed committed even when things seemed darkest. How can examples, such as this man who suffered so much at the hands of others, give us hope in our own committed lives to God?

.... Notes ....

D......Devout Prayer Life

"Pray without ceasing." 1 Thess. 5:17

There is one way to keep Christ near to us throughout every day and to help us grow stronger: speak to Him often in prayer! The ability to pray to God allows us to commune with Him on a personal level and to enhance the father and child relationship He wants to have with each and every person. Paul realized how important prayer was to the Christian life when he wrote to the church at Thessalonica to "pray without ceasing." It is an honor and privilege we share as His children to be able to come before His throne and speak to Him directly about whatever is going on in our lives, to tell Him of our troubles or thank Him for our blessings.

Examples of Prayerful People!
The Bible is full of examples of people who spoke with God often and the effects it had on their lives. We read of the prayers of Abraham through his life of trials and wandering. Not only can we read of Abraham's prayers, but in Genesis 24:1-15, we can see that Abraham's servant was impacted by his master's example as he prays for God's blessing in choosing a wife for Isaac.

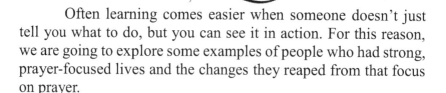

Often learning comes easier when someone doesn't just tell you what to do, but you can see it in action. For this reason, we are going to explore some examples of people who had strong, prayer-focused lives and the changes they reaped from that focus on prayer.

Daniel – Daniel 6

From a very young age, we learn how Daniel was a man of God, concerned with living God's way. Whether it was refusing to defile himself by eating the king's delicacies or waiting on God for the interpretation of the king's dreams, Daniel trusted in God's ways to guide him through life.

One of the ways Daniel stayed so faithful to God was through his steadfast dedication to prayer. Daniel stayed connected to God by speaking with him often. In Daniel 6, we learn not just that he had been made the governor, but that he was distinguished among the governors and satraps (local rulers) appointed in the land. Because of his high appointment, Daniel became the focus of a plot to get rid of him.

Knowing that Daniel was faithful to the habit of prayer (verse 13), the other governors used it against him, deceiving the king into signing a law forbidding prayer to any but him. Daniel did not let this deceitful law stop him from opening up his heart to the Lord, and for his faithfulness to prayer, he was given a death sentence: thrown to the lions.

Even being thrown into the den of lions did not hinder his prayers, but strengthened his faith and the faith of all who witnessed the fantastic saving power of God! Due to Daniel's faithful prayers, the king and all the nation turned toward God.

Hannah – 1 Samuel 1:6-18

Hannah lived a troubled life for years. Although loved desperately by her husband, she was barren and her heart broke for a child. She was also ridiculed and provoked by her sister wife because of her condition. When they would travel to the temple year after year, she would become depressed because of her situation, despite the faithful love of her husband.

In her sorrow, she turned to God in pain so deep that she

couldn't even speak the words aloud, but quietly and fervently, she took it all to the Lord (verse 15-16). When the priest reassured her that God heard her prayers and would answer, she fully trusted that it would be so. The text says she went away *"and her face was no longer sad." (vs. 18)*

Hannah knew who to take her troubles to and to trust Him with the results. She was faithful that her prayers would be answered in God's time.

Paul – Acts 16

There are so many examples of the importance of prayer in Paul's life. There are examples of his praying for the different churches in his epistles, requesting prayers on his behalf, or encouraging the prayers of others. The most moving example of prayer in his life comes at one of his darkest times, his imprisonment.

Instead of sitting in prison focusing on how things were going wrong with his life at the moment, he chose to use the time praying to God and singing praise to His name. The example set by him and Silas for the other prisoners was remarkable. It changed the lives of all who witnessed it, especially the jailor guarding them!

Jesus

Our Lord Jesus is our most magnificent example of many things in life, and prayer is no exception. Jesus constantly took time out in His life to speak to the Father. His prayer life was so evident that His apostles asked Him to teach them to pray as He did (Matt. 6:5-15).

On many occasions, He sought a few moments alone from the crowds that followed Him to reconnect with the Father. There were even times He would spend all night in prayer (Luke 6:12). He prayed while in such agony that His sweat became as drops of blood (Luke 22:44).

One of the most beautiful examples of a prayer of Jesus is found in John 17. Jesus spends a small moment praying for Himself and the trials He is about to endure. He then prays for His disciples, for their strength and protection in a world they will have to soon face without Him. Finally, He prays for you and me, all those who would believe in the apostle's words. How amazing that in one of His darkest hours, our Lord and Savior took the time to remember us in prayer before the Father.

In Jesus' limited time on Earth, He always found time to speak with the Father, and this is the example we must follow in our own lives. As we desire to grow stronger in our personal spiritual walk with God, we must not neglect time with our Lord.

Types of Prayers

Prayer is a conversation with God. Too often, we look at prayer as more complicated than it has to be, and it brings a false feeling of inability to our hearts. Prayer should be as simple as talking to the person sitting next to you; but realize that, though He desires us to come before His throne any and every time we will, we must approach the Lord with the respect and adoration due Him.

As Paul wrote to the church in Thessalonica, prayer should be made without ceasing (1 Thessalonians 5:16-18),

"Rejoice always, pray without ceasing, in everything give thanks; for this is the will of God in Christ Jesus for you."

It is the will of God in His Son that we bring Him everything that we face in our lives, during the good times and the bad. As we grow in our love for Jesus Christ, we will naturally desire to talk to Him. He already knows every thought and desire of our heart, but His desire is for us to bring it willingly and lay it at His feet, placing our cares in His capable hands.

Prayer is more than asking for God's help with illness and grief. It is more than thanking Him for the blessings He bestows. In 1 Timothy 2:1, Paul gives us four of the main types of prayers.

"Therefore, I exhort first of all that supplications, prayers, intercessions, and giving of thanks be made for all men,"

Supplication

Prayers of supplication are when we take requests to God.

62

These are when we lay at His feet all the things that are troubling in our lives. All the cares and worries of our life that we are struggling to process and understand are presented to Him for Him to take care of as He sees appropriate.

Philippians 4:6 tells us, *"Do not be anxious about anything, but in everything by prayer and supplication with thanksgiving let your requests be made known to God."* We should not be troubled about the things of this life but should take them to God, trusting in His promises to hear our cry and take care of our needs.

Prayers

This word covers it all, any conversation with God from requesting His help and guidance to offering Him your thankfulness for the blessings in your life. Anytime you talk with God, you are offering up prayers to Him.

Jesus summed up prayer simply in Matthew 7:7 when He said, *"Ask, and it will be given to you seek, and you will find; knock, and it will be opened to you."*

Intercession

Intercessory prayers are those we offer up on behalf of another. Maybe we are praying for the physical health of a family member. Perhaps we are lifting a friend up for strength through a tough time in his or her life. Any time we "intercede" for others, we are asking God to be with them. These prayers are important and special. Never underestimate the power of lifting up someone's name to our Lord and Savior.

Paul wrote, in 1 Timothy 2:1, for us to make intercession for all men. There are few things as powerful as taking the name of another to God with a heart of love and care. Jesus spent most of His prayer in John 17 on behalf of His apostles; we too should constantly be lifting up those in our lives to the Father.

Prayers of Thanksgiving

Recognizing all God has done in our lives is essential. We must be open and willing to take time from our schedules, not to ask Him for anything, but to merely acknowledge Him and say thank you. David wrote in Psalm 95:2, *"Let us come into his presence with thanksgiving; let us make a joyful noise to him with songs of praise!"*

God is the giver of all blessings, and we need to remember and take time out to thank Him for all He does for us.

Tips for Praying Biblically

I firmly believe you would not be taking this journey toward a stronger spiritual life if you did not truly want this for yourself. As you seek to improve your prayer life, take these tips from the Word for growing your daily prayer time; may they give focus and dedication to your conversation with God.

Psalm 55:17 - Pray at any time!
"Evening and morning and at noon I will pray, and cry aloud, And He shall hear my voice."

We are blessed that there is no set time or place for us to approach God in prayer. Be willing at any and every opportunity you have to open your heart to God and share with Him your concerns.

1 Peter 4:7 - Be Serious and Watchful in our prayers.
"But the end of all things is at hand; therefore, be serious and watchful in your prayers."

While we are blessed with the ability to come before God anytime we can, we must remember that we are praying to the Lord and Creator, the King of Kings. Our prayers must not be offered up half-heartedly but must be in seriousness of heart and mind, with our focus being on Him only. We must be reverent to the Lord we serve and wholly aware of the honor it is that we can pray to Him freely.

1 John 5:14 - Pray to God with Confidence
"Now this is the confidence that we have in Him, that if we ask anything according to His will, He hears us."

Pray to the Lord with full assurance that He hears your heartfelt needs. We do not have to worry about God being too busy to hear our pleas. God is always available, day or night, and we can be assured that our prayers will be heeded with the greatest of concern.

Colossians 4:2 - With Thanksgiving in our hearts

"Continue earnestly in prayer, being vigilant in it with thanksgiving."

While prayers of thanksgiving are something special in and of themselves, we must always have an attitude of thankfulness in our hearts when we approach the Lord. God is the giver of life itself, and we must be constantly aware of His willingness to save and forgive.

Matthew 21:22 - Ask Believing
"And whatever things you ask in prayer, believing, you will receive."

Our prayers must not be uttered with doubt. While God may not answer them in the ways we think they should be answered, we must believe that He is capable of answering our petitions. God is the promise keeper, the all-powerful Lord, and nothing is beyond Him. We must believe that nothing we take to God is too hard or too big for Him to handle.

Matthew 5:44 - Pray for those who Use and Persecute you.

"But I say to you, love your enemies, bless those who curse you, do good to those who hate you, and pray for those who spitefully use you and persecute you."

This is a difficult one for most people, but it is a powerful moment when you can look past the hurt feelings and pray to the Lord for His best for another individual, regardless of what he or she has done. This is reaching a level of seeing a person as God

65

does, as a soul in need of His salvation. Once we can learn to see the souls of others, and not simply their actions, then we can learn to pray for them as Christ prayed for us, even as He hung on the cross.

Power Verse

"Then you will call upon Me and go and pray to Me, and I will listen to you. And you will seek Me and find Me, when you search for Me with all your heart."
Jeremiah 29:12-13

D.......Devout Prayer Life

Worksheet

"Pray without ceasing." 1 Thess. 5:17

Examples of Prayerful People!
Daniel – Daniel 6
What stands out to you about the life of Daniel?

_____
_____
_____
_____

Would people recognize prayer as an important part of your life?

_____
_____
_____
_____

Would your prayer life be an example to lead others to trust in God?

_____
_____
_____
_____

Hannah – 1 Samuel 1:6-18

Do you take your troubles to God in prayer?

_____

_____

_____

_____

Hannah left the care for her prayer with God. How do you trust that He is able to provide and take care of the prayers you lift up to Him?

_____

_____

_____

_____

Paul – Acts 16

When times are hard in life, how are you able to find joy in prayer?

_____

_____

_____

_____

How can you be an example to others through your prayer life during times of trouble and sorrow?

_____

_____

_____

_____

Jesus

Jesus sought the Father at all times of the day. How many ways can you seek out the Lord in prayer during your day?

_____

_____

_____

_____

Do you long for that quiet time with Him in prayer?

_____

_____

Who are some of the people around you that you can remember in prayer?

_____

_____

_____

_____

Types of Prayers
Prayer is a conversation with God.

> *"Rejoice _____, pray without _____, in _____ give thanks; for this is the will of God in Christ Jesus for you." 1 Thess. 5:16-17*

1 Timothy 2:1, Paul gives us four of the main types of prayers.

> *"Therefore, I exhort first of all that _____, _____, _____, and _____ be made for all men," 1 Timothy 2:1*

1. _____
2. _____
3. _____
4. _____

Supplication
Philippians 4:6 *"Do not be _____ about anything, but in everything by prayer and supplication with thanksgiving let your requests be made known to God."*

Prayers
Matthew 7:7 *"_____, and it will be given to you; _____, and you will find; _____, and it will be opened to you."*

69

Intercession
1 Timothy 2:1 for us to make intercession for _____ men.

Prayers of Thanksgiving
    Psalm 95:2, *"Let us come into his presence with
    _____; let us make a joyful noise to him with songs of
    praise!"*

Tips for Praying Biblically
Psalm 55:17 - Pray at any time!
    " _____ and _____ and at _____ I will
    pray, and cry aloud, And He shall hear my voice."

1 Peter 4:7 - Be Serious and Watchful in our prayers.
    *"But the end of all things is at hand; therefore, be _____
    and _____ in your prayers."*

1 John 5:14 - Pray to God with Confidence
    *"Now this is the _____ that we have in Him, that if we
    ask anything according to His will, He _____ us."*

Colossians 4:2 - With Thanksgiving in our hearts
    *"Continue _____ in prayer, being vigilant in it with
    _____."*

Matthew 21:22 - Ask Believing
    *"And whatever things you ask in prayer, _____, you
    will receive."*

Matthew 5:44 - Pray for those who Use and Persecute you.
    *"But I say to you, _____ your enemies, bless those who
    _____ you, do _____ to those who hate you, and pray for
    those who spitefully use you and persecute you."*

Daily Prayer and Journal Starters

Day 1 – Jeremiah 33:3
It is a comforting thought to know that when we need help, it is only a phone call away. God is even closer, even more dependable, and you never need a phone to reach Him. There is no worrying about a wrong number or a busy signal. God is always available to hear our prayers. Think of times in your day when you could really use someone to talk to. How would opening your heart to God regularly unburden your heart?

Day 2 – Romans 12:9-13
This short list holds characteristics for Christian behavior. In its midst, the Holy Spirit is telling us to continue steadfastly in prayer. A Christian's life requires a continual conversation with our Lord and Creator. Think of how many conversations you carry on during the course of a day. Shouldn't God get as much of your attention? If you talk to the person you are closest to for the same amount of time you speak with God, how would that relationship develop? Would it grow stronger?

Day 3 – Ephesians 6:10-18
The Bible tells us of the armor which give us protection from the temptations this world throws at us. At the end of the passage, notice the importance of prayer in our spiritual defense. We are told to pray always and be watchful. Prayer can strengthen our resolve to follow Christ no matter what the circumstances. Think of areas in your life where you feel weak or where you are struggling. In what ways can you ask for God's help to keep you strong? List some ways in which you could use God's support.

Day 4 – Psalm 4:1
David constantly bowed before God, pleading for His assistance and protection. He also recognized when God answered his

prayers. Think back to prayers God has answered for you. Was the answer what you had imagined? Write a thank you letter to God for His answered prayers.

Day 5 – Psalm 145:18

God is near to all who call upon Him in truth. We must realize how important it is to approach God, knowing the truth of what He has promised. God has not promised earthly wealth or fame, nor a life of ease. Instead, God has promised us every spiritual blessing in Christ Jesus. What promises of God would you spend time in prayer about?

Day 6 – Daniel 6:10

Daniel did not change his pattern of prayer, even in the face of persecution. This is a devoted prayer life. Think of your personal prayer life. Are you consistent? Do people ask you to pray for them? Do you remember to do it later or forget? Daniel knew that prayer is powerful, and he routinely bowed before God. Do you feel prayer is a powerful tool in your life?

Day 7 – Acts 2:42

In the first days of Christ's church, Christian brothers and sisters continued steadfastly in prayer. Praying together is powerful. Think of people in your life with whom you could join together in prayer. How would your relationship change with others when you unite in prayer? As you discuss and reach out to God about things that are important in your life, will it bring you closer?

Deeper Study

Read the following prayers: 1 Kings 8:22-30; 2 Kings 19:15-19; Ezra 9:5-15; Isaiah 38:2-8; and Luke 18:13. Think about the purpose and feeling behind each prayer. What type of prayers are they? Think of other prayers in Scripture. What similarities do you see? What differences? What can you learn from these for your own prayers?

E.......Encourage Others

"Therefore encourage each other and edify one another just as you also were doing." 1 Thessalonians 5:11

James states, in James 2:17, that faith without works is dead. As you struggle to strengthen your own spiritual life, the best opportunity for growth comes when it is put into action. If you want to gain strength in your physical muscles, you must work them out regularly. Miss a few days of your workout, and you can feel the difference it makes in strength.

Your spiritual strength is no different and must also be exercised regularly. For it to grow and develop, it must be pushed often and used to grow deeper and stronger. A powerful way to grow your spiritual life is to encourage another person in their spiritual walk with God.

Encouraging others is a powerful biblical principle. In 1 Thessalonians 5:11, Paul wrote to the church in Thessalonica, saying, *"Therefore encourage each other and edify one another just as you also were doing."* He saw the good work they were doing in lifting one another up and urged them to continue in their encouraging ways. Paul knew the abundant relationship connections that encouragement helps to build in the church

and in individual lives. He knew the power it would bring to everyone in their walk with God.

Encouraging Examples

Regarding how we are to walk with God, the Bible doesn't just tell us how to live, it shows us. There are people whose lives are detailed throughout the pages of God's Word who show us how to be encouragers of one another. Their lives help us understand how to raise up and strengthen the spiritual lives of our brothers and sisters.

Joses – Acts 4:36

Most of us would not recognize the name Joses, yet we recognize the "nickname" he was given by the apostles: Barnabas.

"And Joses, who was also named Barnabas by the apostles (which is translated Son of Encouragement), a Levite of the country of Cyprus, having land, sold it, and brought the money and laid it at the apostles' feet." Acts 4:36-37

Barnabas was a man who did anything he could to encourage others and to make it possible for the brothers and sisters around him to grow stronger in their relationships with God.

Early in the foundation of the church, people had traveled from many nations to Jerusalem. As the days drew out, those people were struggling to afford to be able to continue to stay in the city to worship and learn (Acts 2-4). It is in this time of need when we learn of people like Barnabas, who were doing all they could to make it possible for them to remain in that location.

Barnabas made such an impact in encouraging others in their spiritual walk that his name was changed to reflect his lifestyle. His encouraging works, however, did not stop there in Jerusalem.

Later in the book of Acts, Barnabas is one being sent from Jerusalem to distant cities to encourage the Christians who had been scattered after the death of Stephen. Look at the effect an encouraging individual can have on the faith of others.

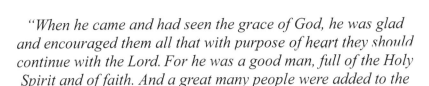

"When he came and had seen the grace of God, he was glad and encouraged them all that with purpose of heart they should continue with the Lord. For he was a good man, full of the Holy Spirit and of faith. And a great many people were added to the Lord." Acts 11:23-24

Barnabas had the gift of encouragement, and he shared it freely. I have no doubt that the sharing of this gift equally served to keep Barnabas himself encouraged and strengthened as he saw those around him growing in their faith. Sharing his gift grew his own purpose of heart to continue in this path for the Lord.

While no one is going to become a Barnabas overnight, each day we can take steps to grow in this area by looking for opportunities to encourage even just one person. Every day growth can occur in our own spiritual walk as we seek out those moments to offer a word of encouragement to another.

Paul – 2 Corinthians 12:19b, 13:10-11

Paul is another strong example of an encourager to many in the New Testament. Paul encouraged through his writings and his visits, which we read about in the book of Acts. In 2 Corinthians 12:19b, Paul wrote, *"We do all things, beloved, for your edification."* One of his major purposes, aside from the spreading of the Gospel of Christ, was to encourage Christians in that Gospel truth they had learned.

Paul encourages Christians to remain not only strong in their faith but strong against temptation. He warns the Christians at Corinth that not all things edify and encourage, but they were to seek out the wellbeing of those around them.

"All things are lawful for me, but not all things are helpful; all things are lawful for me, but not all things edify. Let no one seek his own, but each one the other's well-being." 1 Cor. 10:23-24

Encouraging others in the things that are going to be good for their spiritual well-being will likewise be good for our own.

75

Ultimately, Paul sought to encourage them to see not only their growth but the growth of the church family. We can see this attitude reflected in Hebrews 10:24-25.

> *"And let us consider one another in order to stir up love and good works, not forsaking the assembling of ourselves together, as is the manner of some, but exhorting one another, and so much the more as you see the Day approaching."*

One blessing of meeting together with the church is so each member of the Lord's body can encourage one another. Paul saw this, and he worked toward this on his missionary journeys. He revisited different cities, "strengthening the churches" (Acts 15:41) in their faith (Acts 16:5) and "encouraging them with many words" (Acts 20:2). Paul knew that encouragement was important to a strong spiritual life.

Who Are We to Encourage?

Once we see the power of encouragement, who do we share that power with? Are there certain ones God desires us to lift up with our words and actions, ones that maybe we would not normally consider? God instructs us to encourage several different types of people throughout Scripture.

Our Leaders and Those in Authority

Those who are in places of authority are not only in places of power but also hold stresses and concerns that many of us cannot imagine. Their struggles are different and hold more impact since the choices they make affect not only their own lives but the lives of all those they rule. For these reasons and more, God expects us to offer encouragement to those in leadership positions.

Deut. 1:38 - At the end of Moses' life, he instructed the children of Israel to encourage Joshua as he took over as their leader to take them into the Promised Land. God, Himself, even commanded Moses to encourage Joshua as he was about to lead the children of Israel through the next stage of their journey (Deut. 3:28).

Exodus 18 – When Moses was leading the children of Israel, he too received encouragement. Jethro, the priest of Midian, Moses' father-in-law, encouraged him to break down the leadership of the people into levels where he would not be so exhausted by the amount of work before him.

You can also note God's attitude toward those in positions of authority by reading Romans 13:1-7.

Our Spiritual Leaders and Those Dedicated to His Service

Those who dedicate their lives to the work and study in God's kingdom deserve our encouragement, whether leaders in our congregations or missionaries around the world. Those who have chosen to serve in these roles are responsible for the spiritual well-being of those in their care and will be held to a higher standard by God. Their roles are difficult, filled with a heartfelt concern for the souls around them.

2 Chronicles 31:4 - In the Old Testament, special arrangements were made for the people to contribute support for the Levites and priests. These men were to dedicate their lives to God and spend them doing His work, not to be concerned with having to work to support their families. This allowed them to be fully devoted to His service. The support from the people around them is what allowed them to continually serve in every way.

2 Chronicles 35:2 - After the word of God was found in the temple and King Josiah restored true worship back to the kingdom, he set them in their duties and encouraged them in their service to the Lord.

2 Chronicles 30:22 - We have an example given of King Hezekiah, as he celebrated the Passover feast, offering encouragement to all the Levites who taught the good knowledge of the Lord.

Paul's letters in the New Testament are full of encouragement for individuals, as well as whole congregations, fellow ministers, and Christians who were dedicated to spreading the message of Christ. Examples can be found in Ephesians 6:21-22 [individuals] beloved brother & faithful minister; and Philippians 1:3-8 [church]. Paul was also encouraged to hear from the churches (Phil. 2:19).

One Another

Romans 15:1-6 - Instructions are given by Paul concerning encouraging others, with the ultimate result of glorifying God. While we are strong and capable, we are to lift others up and do good that leads to edification. Then when we are at our weak moments, they will be able to encourage and lift us up!

The Church

We are to seek to excel so that the church is encouraged and grows, but not just for our own pride. It should be for the edification of God's body!

"Even so you, since you are zealous for spiritual gifts, let it be for the edification of the church that you seek to excel."
1 Corinthians 14:12

In fact, Paul tells the Christians in Corinth that everything he did was to lift them up. Paul knew that an encouraged people were a people strong enough to withstand the pressures of this world and the discouragement that fear and doubt can bring.

"Again, do you think that we excuse ourselves to you? We speak before God in Christ. But we do all things, beloved, for your edification." *2 Corinthians 12:19*

How to Encourage...

God equips all His children, so they are prepared to do their part in His kingdom. Each of us is equipped to do what God knows we will be best at, whether that is encouraging or teaching, singing or praying. God gives us the skills we all need.

Paul writes, in Ephesians 4:12-16, of some of the gifts that Christians have for the service of God. He states that the gifts are given by God to each person *"for the equipping of the saints for the work of ministry."* The *work* of ministry shows that God intends these gifts to be used and exercised. God does not merely give a gift but gives us help in how to use the gift of encouragement. As with any gift that God bestows, there are

certain expectations and ways in which God desires for us to use it to His glory.

We are to Speak Only Words that Edify!

"Let no corrupt word proceed out of your mouth, but what is good for necessary edification, that it may impart <u>grace</u> to the <u>hearer</u>." Ephesians 4:29

Words are powerful, and God knows it! He warns time and again about watching what we say. James warns of the unbridled tongue. God wants us speaking to others that which will lift and encourage them in their walk of life. Paul goes on to tell us that we are told to stay away from evil speaking (Eph. 4:31).

Scriptures such as 1 Timothy 1:4 tell us to stay away from things that do not lead to edification. We are all aware of the dangers of hurtful words, gossip, and lies that do nothing but tear down a person to his or her core. We are to speak what God would have us speak, that which is positive and uplifting, and to pay no attention to the rest!

Offer Encouragement in Times of Trial

We all face hard times; no life is without its troubles. We need to be open and willing to offer support and encouragement to others when they are enduring such times!

2 Chronicles 32 has a wonderful example of encouragement. The king of Assyria had entered Judah, and King Hezekiah offers encouragement to the people as they prepare for the enemy (verse 6). It is during such hard times in life when some people will finally become open to the words of God.

Another such hardship facing the children of Israel is found in Isaiah.

"Everyone helped his neighbor, and said to his brother, "Be of good courage!" So the craftsman <u>encouraged</u> the goldsmith; he who smooths with the hammer <u>inspired</u> him who strikes the anvil," Isaiah 41:6-7a

This verse sounds wonderful. How great to think that they were offering such encouragement to one another! Unfortunately, this was a "satire" for the Israelites, describing how the enemy was joining together to make "powerful" idols to come against God. This was not saying that they were encouraging one another in the worship of the true God! However, it was used to illustrate that God, the one and only powerful and True Lord, was on Israel's side when they needed this assurance the most.

Offer Only Sincere Encouragement

Sometimes it is so tempting to say things just because we think it is what a person would like to hear. We must be careful of this and make sure that when we offer someone words of encouragement, those words are sincere. Our words must come from our heart, with real feeling behind them. May we not offer words just for others to hear, even if we think at the moment it is easier.

In 1 Kings 22:13-28, there is an example of the kings of Israel and Judah seeking Micaiah for a prophecy. They wanted him to speak words of encouragement just as the other "wise men" had offered them. The other so-called prophets were telling the kings what they wanted to hear to keep their jobs. But Micaiah could not do that. He could only speak the words God gave him to say. Although the words may not have seemed encouraging because it wasn't the desired response, words of truth, when accepted and considered, will bring more encouragement to life than simple flattery.

We must be careful not to fall into that trap! People would much rather hear words from the heart! Let us grow stronger in offering real encouragement to those around us. Solomon wrote how powerful an uplifting word can be in the heart and life of one who is struggling when he said, *"Anxiety in the heart of man causes depression, but a good word makes it glad"* (Proverbs 12:25). Let us help make the hearts of those around us glad!

Power Verse

"I have shown you in every way, by laboring like this, that you must support the weak. And remember the words of the Lord Jesus, that He said, 'It is more blessed to give than to receive.'"
Acts 20:35

E.......Encourage

Others

Worksheet

"Therefore encourage each other and edify one another just as you also were doing." 1 Thessalonians 5:11

Encouraging Examples
Joses – Acts 4:36 (Barnabas)
"And Joses, who was also named Barnabas by the apostles (which is translated _____ _____ _____)..."
Acts 4:36

Think of someone who has been a Barnabas in your life. Describe how their words or actions have made an impact.

_____
_____
_____
_____

"When he came and had seen the grace of God, he was glad, and _____ them all that with _____ of heart they should continue with the Lord. For he was a good man, full of the Holy Spirit and of faith. And a great many people were added to the Lord." Acts 11:23-24

Barnabas purposed in his heart to encourage others. When life gets hard and stress builds up, describe how important is it to have

82

a heart set with the purpose of encouraging others.

_____

_____

_____

_____

Paul – 2 Corinthians 12:19b, 13:10-11
"We do all things, beloved, for your _____."
2 Corinthians 12:19b

Everything Paul did was with this purpose: the spreading of the Gospel and encouraging Christians. If you purposed in your heart to encourage others each morning, would your day look any different?

_____

_____

_____

_____

> *"All things are lawful for me, but not all things are*
> *_____; all things are lawful for me, but not all things*
> *_____. Let no one seek his own, but _____ one the*
> *_____ well-being." 1 Cor. 10:23-24*

Describe how you could seek the well-being of another in your day.

_____

_____

_____

> *"And let us _____ one another in order to stir up love*
> *and good works, not forsaking the assembling of ourselves*
> *together, as is the manner of some, but _____ one*
> *another, and so much the more as you see the Day*
> *approaching." Hebrews 10:24-25*

How would truly considering one another before acting or speaking change how you acted and reacted?

83

_____

_____
_____
_____
_____

Who Are We to Encourage?

Our Leaders and Those in Authority
Our leaders are often in tough situations; think of ways you can offer encouragement and support much like the people were instructed to encourage Joshua. List some of the ideas and find ways to carry them out to your local leaders.

_____
_____
_____
_____

Our Spiritual Leaders and Those Dedicated to His Service
"I _____ my God upon every remembrance of _____."
Philippians 1:3

Pray for those spiritual leaders around you, but don't stop there. Encourage those leaders by letting them know they are in your prayers. Ask them if they need prayers in specific areas in their lives. Make a list of names of the spiritual leaders (elders, deacons, preachers, missionaries, etc.) in your circle and say a special prayer for them.

_____
_____
_____
_____

One Another
Look again at the instructions given in Romans 15:1-7. Think of those around you who are struggling and think of ways you can offer them encouragement.

_____
_____

The Church

"Even so you, since you are zealous for spiritual gifts, let it be for the _____ of the church that you seek to excel."
1 Corinthians 14:12

Think of your local congregation of the Lord's body. What ways could the church use encouragement? How could you offer your gifts and talents to strengthen the body?

_____

_____

_____

How To Encourage...

"for the _____ of the saints for the _____ of ministry." Ephesians 4:12

What gifts/opportunities for service did Paul mention in this section of Scripture?

_____

_____

_____

Including encouraging others, list more ways you can serve God and His kingdom.

_____

_____

_____

_____

We are to Speak Only Words that Edify!

"Let no _____ word proceed out of your mouth, but what is _____ for necessary _____, that it may impart _____ to the hearer." Ephesians 4:29

"Let all bitterness, wrath, anger, clamor, and evil speaking be _____ _____ _____ _____, *with all malice. And* _____ _____ *to one another, tenderhearted, forgiving one another, even as God in Christ forgave you." Ephesians 4:31-32*

The words we choose have a powerful impact on others. How can your words be used to encourage another when the situation is less than pleasant?

_____

_____

_____

_____

Offer Encouragement in Times of Trial

"and gave them _____, *saying, 'Be strong and courageous.'" 2 Chronicles 32:6b-7a*

Read on through verse 8 of that chapter. What words did Hezekiah use to offer the most encouragement to the people? How can you encourage others using the line of thinking that help is from the Lord?

_____

_____

_____

_____

Offer Only Sincere Encouragement

False encouragement can be easily detected. Think of times when it would be easy to use the words someone wants to hear, rather than the words they need to hear. Think of ways to carefully use sincere encouragement.

_____

_____

_____

_____

"Anxiety in the heart of man causes _____, *but a good word makes it* _____*." Proverbs 12:25*

Daily Prayer and Journal Starters

Day 1 – Acts 20:35

We are called to support those around us who are weak. This weakness can come in many forms: emotional, financial, physical, and spiritual. We can give encouragement to lighten the burden of others and help them grow closer to God in their lives. It is a true statement that it is more blessed to give than to receive. To lay encouraging words on another and see them lifted will lift you and help you become more like our Lord. Make a list of people in your life you could offer encouragement and help to this week.

Day 2 – Ephesians 4:29

The ability to encourage others begins with basic communication skills: how you express your thoughts to others. In everyday speech, are your words helpful or hurtful? Imagine someone is recording your conversations. How would you feel hearing the playback? Were your words angry, coarse, and rough? Were they soft and gentle? Would you want someone speaking like that to you? To your spouse? To your children? Think about how you can be more aware of your words in daily conversations.

Day 3 – 1 Samuel 23:16

Do you encourage others through God? Do you seek out friends who will encourage you through God? Godly friends can help each other in their walks toward the Lord. Do you have friends in your circle whom you can turn to for godly support? Who could you depend on for encouragement when times are difficult in your life? Are others able to depend on you for this kind of

encouragement? How does it make you feel to receive godly encouragement?

Day 4 – Proverbs 16:24

Words are powerful. They can bring us joy or break us down. Today seek out opportunities to use your words to bring sweetness to another's life. Look for any positive reactions your words bring. Pay attention to the way the words others use and how they make you feel in response. Are you surrounding yourself with people who are encouraging you?

Day 5 – Proverbs 12:25

Everyone suffers from something. We all deal with some level of anxiety and stress in our lives. When we allow the hurtful words of others to sink into our hearts, we can begin to believe lies about ourselves. Keep the truth of God in your heart and allow it to bring you peace while dispelling the hurtful words of others. What is a truth from God that you find comforting when the words from another sting?

Day 6 – Proverbs 25:11

Words spoken to us are hard to forget, good or bad; nor is it easy to forget how those words make us feel. Kind and encouraging words are like fine jewelry adorning our hearts. We wear them proudly. Think of words which have encouraged you, words that lifted your spirit. Remember them and wear them with honor. Think today of how you can embellish someone else's life with the same kind of words. Give them something they can think back on fondly when they are having a hard time.

Day 7 – Hebrews 3:13a

Don't put off saying good words! Encouraging others should be a daily occurrence, while it is called *today*. We are called by our Creator to lift one another up, and we do not need to wait. Do not procrastinate this command saying, "It's not the right time," or "Today is not good; tomorrow will be better." Even if your day is not going well, try speaking kind words to others and see the difference it makes in your own life. There is

power in encouraging others. Try this for a few days and record what effects you notice in your own life.

Deeper Study

Read Acts 4:36. Consider what kind of life a man named Joses must have lived. Those he was surrounded by called him "Barnabas" meaning "son of encouragement." What kind of life must he have led? What kind of activities would you imagine him involved with? What would others call you? What would you need to do in your life for others to call you a "daughter of encouragement?" Read through the book of Acts and look for other times when Barnabas is mentioned. What events are surrounding him in those moments?

.... Notes ....

F.... Faith:

A Firm Foundation

"For no other foundation can anyone lay than that which is laid, which is Jesus Christ." 1 Corinthians 3:11

In today's chaotic world, people set their faith and hope in many different places. Faith is placed in job security, in money saved, in getting that lucky lottery ticket, or in wishing upon a star, but less and less are people placing it where it deserves to be: in God. The only place faith can make a difference is when it is placed in our Lord and Father in heaven.

This world is constantly changing. It is uncertain and unstable, nothing is sure; however, God is steady and firm. Faith in Him gives you sure footing in the shifting sands of this life, and everyone needs something to cling to when life becomes rough and uneven. To survive the craziness and not become overturned in the sea of uncertainty, faith in God is necessary for a strong spiritual life, as well as for a strong and stable physical and emotional life.

The definition of *faith* from God's Word is what we are concerned with in this chapter, and it is much different from the world's view of faith. Hebrews 11:1 explains for us part of God's idea of faith, saying, *"Now faith is the substance of things hoped for, the evidence of things not seen."* Faith is the reason we have hope; it is our evidence for the things we cannot see with our physical eyes.

What is Godly Faith?

The world has a distinct idea of faith. Worldly faith is defined as a confidence or trust placed in a person or thing. Faith is talked about as being in a person or organization's ability. However, according to the world, faith is typically just a belief that is not based on proof, but most of the time on blind acceptance, primarily when the world discusses a religious faith.

Unlike the world's belief, however, God has not called His children to blind faith. In fact, Scripture is not even set up that way. God has shown us many times, from the creation until now, why we can have faith in Him, why we can trust Him completely. Even though He did not have to, He has proved Himself to humanity repeatedly so that we may believe in Him.

While there are too many examples of this to cover in this chapter, there are a few examples of this type of godly faith that will show what I mean. One includes the Christians who were in the city of Berea, who were commended in Acts 17:11 for searching the Scriptures daily to see of the things they were being told were true. It was a praiseworthy attribute that they did not just take the words that were being spoken to them and blindly accept them, but they looked back into God's Word and made sure the words were true.

"These were more fair-minded than those in Thessalonica, in that they received the word with all readiness, and searched the Scriptures daily to find out whether these things were so."

The apostle Luke penned his letters of Luke and Acts to Theophilus in such a way—including specific names and locations—that the accounts he recorded could be verified by Theophilus. In fact, Luke goes so far as to write that while these things were from eyewitnesses and ministers of the word of God, he still wanted an orderly account so, *"that you may know."* He wanted to show Theophilus as much proof as possible so his faith in what was being taught would be strong.

"It seemed good to me also, having had perfect understanding of all things from the very first, to write to you an orderly account, most excellent Theophilus, that you may know the certainty of those things in which you were instructed." Luke 1:3-4

Jesus Himself came not just with powerful words to encourage faithfulness, but with signs and wonders to prove that what He was saying was true and that He was indeed the Son of God. (See what God had to say about Jesus in Hebrews 2.) His disciples carried this same style of teaching onward and Mark 16:20 records that they confirmed the Word with accompanying signs.

"And they went out and preached everywhere, the Lord working with them and confirming the word through the accompanying signs. Amen." Mark 16:20

Yes, God wants full faith from us, but not a blind faith. NO! It is a faith that has been confirmed over and over again across centuries from a multitude of locations and a wide variety of people. God desires our faith to be strong, nothing doubted, so that we can trust Him, follow Him, and believe His promises.

Why is Faith Foundational?

As Christians, children of God, and believers of the Most High God, our faith in Him is foundational to everything concerning our relationship with God. It is the very thing we build on and grow in. In our very salvation, we are to hear the Word and believe (John 12:46-47; Acts 4:4; and Acts 18:8 are just a few examples).

Our faith in God is what drives us to act, living obediently to Him. Hebrews 11 is a chapter full of examples, which Hebrews 12:1-2 calls a great cloud of witnesses, of people who acted on their faith, who did what God asked of them and lived their lives for Him. These people did not merely have faith, but they had faith so strong that it drove them to action.

The author of Hebrews also points out, *"But without faith*

it is impossible to please Him, for he who comes to God must believe that He is, and that He is a rewarder of those who diligently seek Him." (Hebrews 11:6). Without our faith, we cannot be found pleasing to God because it is that faith that will drive us to live as the examples in that chapter lived.

James also brings out some of these examples of heroes of great faith in James, chapter 2. He points out how their faith led them to act on what God had commanded them. He also includes a compelling statement that shows how important this kind of live and active faith is to the Christian life.

> *"But do you want to know, O foolish man, that faith without works is dead?" James 2:20*

Our faith must be an active, obedient faith; it is a faith that we can grow in and serve with. It cannot be faith in word only. Our faith must be built upon with all diligence, as Peter writes in 2 Peter 1:5-7,

> *"But also for this very reason, giving all diligence, add to your faith virtue, to virtue knowledge, to knowledge self-control, to self-control perseverance, to perseverance godliness, to godliness brotherly kindness, and to brotherly kindness love."*

Our faith is foundational because it is what we build on. Look at what Peter wrote, that we are to take our faith, our foundation, and add to it virtue, then knowledge, then self-control, and so on. Each block builds on the last and makes our spiritual lives even stronger, one step at a time, one block at a time, starting with our faith. If we build on our faith in such a way, we are promised something in verse 8.

> *"For if these things are yours and abound, you will be neither barren nor unfruitful in the knowledge of our Lord Jesus Christ."*

If we build these things onto our faith, then we have the promise that we will not be barren or unfruitful in the knowledge of Christ. We will never be empty. We will never be unproductive

in His kingdom, and in our own lives, because we will be living our faith, acting on it, and obeying Him through it.

Where Faith Belongs

If our faith is so essential and so foundational to our Christian walk, then it is important to know what to have faith in, what our faith belongs in, so we may have the right kind of faith, the faith like those described in Hebrews 11. First, we must realize that there is only one true faith. There is only one God and one true faith in that God. God is strong in the power of one.

"There is one body and one Spirit, just as you were called in one hope of your calling; one Lord, <u>one faith</u>, one baptism; one God and Father of all, who is above all, and through all, and in you all." Ephesians 4:4-6

Our faith must start with the one God and Him alone. Look at how many times in those three verses He uses the word *one*. Jude emphasized the importance of the singular faith when he wrote in verse 3,

"Beloved, while I was very diligent to write to you concerning our common salvation, I found it necessary to write to you exhorting you to contend earnestly for <u>the faith</u> which was once for all delivered to the saints."

He explains that while he wanted to write to them and encourage them in their common salvation—common meaning that they were unified in one salvation—he found it necessary, because of some of the problems they were having, to encourage them to fight, or contend, for <u>the</u> faith, the one singular faith that was delivered once for all. God wants us to be unified and thus strengthened in that unity of faith.

We cannot place our faith in mankind, in their many theories, in their knowledge, in man's anything when it comes to our salvation. Our faith must be in the only One who has the power to save. 1 Corinthians 2:5 says, "*...that your faith should*

not be in the wisdom of men but in the power of God." Mankind's wisdom through the years does not compare to the power of God to save our souls. We must keep our faith first and foremost in Him.

We must keep faith in the fact that God is faithful. He is the one who keeps His promises. He is the one who will never leave us nor forsake us. 2 Thessalonians 3:3 tells us, *"But the Lord is faithful, who will establish you and guard you from the evil one."* He will establish us and set us up in a permanent way that cannot be shaken or moved. He will guard us, protect us, and keep us from the evil one. Those are compelling reasons for keeping our faith in Him.

Our faith must be in Jesus as the author and finisher of our faith (Hebrews 12:2). He is the One who created everything in the beginning according to John 1:1-3, *"In the beginning was the Word, and the Word was with God, and the Word was God. He was in the beginning with God. All things were made through Him, and without Him nothing was made that was made."* He wrote everything before the foundation of the world (Ephesians 1:4). He carried through with His creation through His sacrifice to the end.

"He then would have had to suffer often since the foundation of the world; but now, once at the end of the ages, He has appeared to put away sin by the sacrifice of Himself." Hebrews 9:26

He put away sin by His sacrifice. With His death, He ended the curse of death for us. He is the finisher of our faith. Our faith belongs in Him.

Our faith belongs in the One who meets our every need.

~**The need for Stability** - Jesus is the One who is unchanging and constant,
"Jesus Christ is the same yesterday, today, and forever."
Hebrews 13:8

~ **The need for a Friend** – Jesus calls us His friend,
"You are My friends if you do whatever I command you. No longer do I call you servants, for a servant does not know what

96

his master is doing; but I have called you friends, for all things that I heard from My Father I have made known to you." John 15:14-15

~The need to be Redeemed to the Father – Jesus is our Redeemer,

"Thus says the Lord, the King of Israel, And his Redeemer, the Lord of hosts: 'I am the First and I am the Last; Besides Me there is no God.'" Isaiah 44:6

~ The need to be Forgiven – Jesus is the forgiver of our sins,

"Him God has exalted to His right hand to be Prince and Savior, to give repentance to Israel and forgiveness of sins." Acts 5:31

~The need to be Delivered – Jesus is our deliverance from death,

"Yes, we had the sentence of death in ourselves, that we should not trust in ourselves but in God who raises the dead, who delivered us from so great a death, and does deliver us; in whom we trust that He will still deliver us." 2 Corinthians 1:9-10

For these reasons and so many more, we can see that Jesus is the One in whom our faith belongs.

Building on our Foundation of Faith

If we want to grow stronger in our spiritual lives, then we must build on our foundation of faith. We have to grow in our faith, feed it, nourish it, and encourage it to reach closer to God every day. How do we do that? How do we grow in our faith and strengthen the foundation that will keep our spiritual lives near to God?

"So then faith comes by hearing, and hearing by the word of God." Romans 10:17

If we want to grow our faith, then we must be in constant connection to the Word of God. Paul reminded the church at Rome that faith came through hearing the Word; the same is true for us.

The fundamental way to strengthen and grow in our faith is to dedicate more time to the study of God's Word. Listen to an audio Bible while you drive; memorize verses of Scripture that you can meditate on during the day; make time to study, even if it is only for a few minutes at a time. You will never regret more time spent listening to what God has to say.

"Having then gifts differing according to the grace that is given to us, let us use them: if prophecy, let us prophesy in proportion to our faith." Romans 12:6

God has given each of us talents. We all have things we can do, and the more we exercise our faith, the stronger it becomes. Just like the muscles of the body grow stronger when we use them and waste away when they are neglected, so is our faith muscle! Use your ability to pray for others. Find someone you can serve and show to them the love of Christ. Send cards and letters of encouragement. Go and sit with the sick or lonely. Bake a cake or cook a meal for someone in need. There are so many ways you can use your gifts to serve God, and in turn, your faith will grow stronger.

"...hearing of your love and faith which you have toward the Lord Jesus and toward all the saints, that the sharing of your faith may become effective by the acknowledgment of every good thing which is in you in Christ Jesus." Philemon 1:5-6

Share your faith! If you want your faith to grow, share it with those around you! Share it by telling others of *every good thing* which is in you because of Christ. Paul was encouraging Philemon to share his faith with those around him, including his new brother in Christ, the returning runaway slave, Onesimus. Sharing our faith keeps us connected to it and connected to the blessings in our life because of Christ. Just like one match lighting a candle doesn't lose its flame, one soul sharing his faith doesn't grow dimmer; instead, they both can grow brighter together!

"...that the genuineness of your faith, being much more precious

than gold that perishes, though it is tested by fire, may be found
to praise, honor, and glory at the revelation of Jesus Christ,"
1 Peter 1:7

Take strength from the knowledge that when your faith is tested, if you stay with God, your faith will be greater on the other side. Peter compares the testing of our faith to the purification of gold. Gold is heated to burn off the impurities that would weaken it over time. Our faith is tested by trial, by temptations, and by the questions, and sometimes even the accusations, of others. But if we hold faith in the things of God that we know to be true, that have been tested through the years and proven, then our shield of faith will protect us!

"...above all, taking the shield of faith with which you will be
able to quench all the fiery darts of the wicked one."
Ephesians 6:16

Know that, in the end, the strengthening of our faith will be reward by God. He will be there, in the end, to congratulate us on a race well run. Our lives, both now and in eternity, will benefit from the efforts of strengthening our faith.

Power Verse

"...receiving the end of your faith—the salvation of your souls."
1 Peter 1:9

F.... Faith:

A Firm Foundation

Worksheet

"For no other foundation can anyone lay than that which is laid, which is Jesus Christ." 1 Corinthians 3:11

What are some of the world's ideas of faith?

_____

_____

_____

How is godly faith different?

_____

_____

_____

"Now faith is the _____ of things hoped for, the _____ of things not seen." Hebrews 11:1

What is Godly Faith?

How are the Christians in Acts 17:11 an example to you?

_____

_____

_____

"These were more fair-minded than those in Thessalonica, in that they received the word with all readiness, and searched the Scriptures _____ to find out whether these things were so."

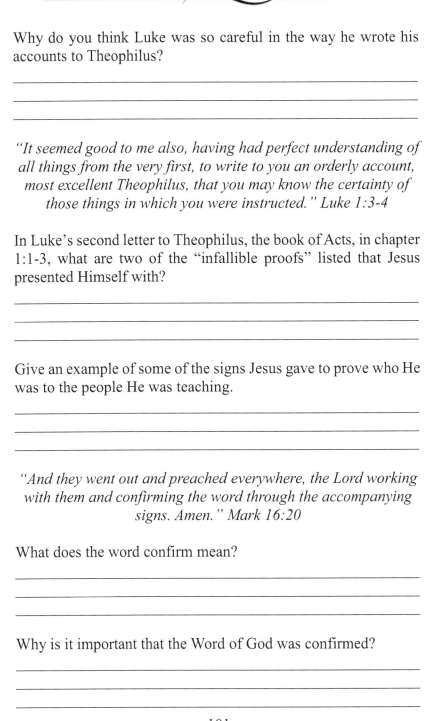

Why do you think Luke was so careful in the way he wrote his accounts to Theophilus?

_____

_____

_____

"It seemed good to me also, having had perfect understanding of all things from the very first, to write to you an orderly account, most excellent Theophilus, that you may know the certainty of those things in which you were instructed." Luke 1:3-4

In Luke's second letter to Theophilus, the book of Acts, in chapter 1:1-3, what are two of the "infallible proofs" listed that Jesus presented Himself with?

_____

_____

_____

Give an example of some of the signs Jesus gave to prove who He was to the people He was teaching.

_____

_____

_____

"And they went out and preached everywhere, the Lord working with them and confirming the word through the accompanying signs. Amen." Mark 16:20

What does the word confirm mean?

_____

_____

_____

Why is it important that the Word of God was confirmed?

_____

_____

_____

Why is Faith Foundational?

Read John 12:46-47; Acts 4:4; and Acts 18:8. What do these passages show you about hearing the Word and believing?

_____

_____

_____

Hebrews 12:1-2 refers to the great cloud of witnesses in chapter 11. Who have been some great examples of faith in your life?

_____

_____

_____

"But without faith it is impossible to please Him, for he who comes to God must believe that He is, and that He is a rewarder of those who diligently seek Him." Hebrews 11:6.

Why do you think it would be impossible to please God without faith?

_____

_____

_____

"But do you want to know, O foolish man, that faith without works is dead?" James 2:20

Look at James 2:14-26. What is James saying about faith?

_____

_____

_____

"But also for this very reason, giving all _____, add to your faith virtue, to virtue knowledge, to knowledge self-control, to self-control perseverance, to perseverance godliness, to godliness brotherly kindness, and to brotherly kindness love."
2 Peter 1:5-7

Think about the different attributes we are to add to our faith in 2 Peter 1:5-7. Think about how each of these could impact your life and write down which ones you feel you need most in your life.

_____

_____

_____

Where Faith Belongs

"There is _____ body and _____ Spirit, just as you were called in _____ hope of your calling; _____ Lord, _____faith, _____ baptism; _____ God and Father of all, who is above all, and through all, and in you all." Ephesians 4:4-6

Thinking about the verse above, and God's desire for unity, read John 17:20-21. What does this idea of being one with Jesus mean to you?

_____

_____

_____

"Beloved, while I was very diligent to write to you concerning our common salvation, I found it necessary to write to you exhorting you to contend earnestly for <u>the faith</u> which was once for all delivered to the saints." Jude 3

While Jude is talking about contending for <u>the</u> faith, think of some challenges that may cause you to need to contend for your beliefs.

_____

_____

_____

"Your faith should not be in the wisdom of men but in the _____ of God." 1 Corinthians 2:5

Think about each of the needs that Jesus fills in our lives and give examples of how this is shown in your own life.

~The need for Stability - *"Jesus Christ is the same yesterday, today, and forever."* Hebrews 13:8

_____

_____

_____

~ The need for a Friend – *"You are My friends if you do whatever I command you. No longer do I call you servants, for a servant does not know what his master is doing; but I have called you friends, for all things that I heard from My Father I have made known to you."* John 15:14-15

_____

_____

_____

~The need to be Redeemed to the Father – *"Thus says the Lord, the King of Israel, And his Redeemer, the Lord of hosts: 'I am the First and I am the Last; Besides Me there is no God."* Isaiah 44:6

_____

_____

_____

~ The need to be Forgiven – *"Him God has exalted to His right hand to be Prince and Savior, to give repentance to Israel and forgiveness of sins."* Acts 5:31

_____

_____

_____

~The need to be Delivered – *"Yes, we had the sentence of death in ourselves, that we should not trust in ourselves but in God who raises the dead, who delivered us from so great a death, and does deliver us; in whom we trust that He will still deliver us."* 2 Corinthians 1:9-10

_____

_____

_____

Think about other areas of life where Jesus fills needs and record them here. Be prayerful and thankful for how Jesus works in your life.

_____

_____

_____

_____

Building on our Foundation of Faith

"So then faith comes by hearing, and hearing by the word of God." Romans 10:17

This chapter lists a few ideas for spending more time each day in God's Word. Use the space below to think about your own life and schedule, and write down more ideas that will work for you.

_____

_____

_____

_____

"Having then gifts differing according to the grace that is given to us, let us use them: if prophecy, let us prophesy in proportion to our faith." Romans 12:6

Think about your own gifts and abilities. Consider the people in your life (friends, co-workers, or family). Name some ways you can use your talents to put your faith into action.

_____

_____

_____

_____

"...hearing of your love and faith which you have toward the Lord Jesus and toward all the saints, that the sharing of your faith may become effective by the acknowledgment of every good thing which is in you in Christ Jesus." Philemon 1:5-6

Name some blessings and good things in your life that you can tell about to share your faith with others.

_____

_____

_____

"...that the genuineness of your faith, being much more precious than gold that perishes, though it is tested by fire, may be found to praise, honor, and glory at the revelation of Jesus Christ,"
1 Peter 1:7

What are some ways your faith has been tested?

_____

_____

_____

"...above all, taking the shield of faith with which you will be able to quench all the fiery darts of the wicked one." Ephesians 6:16

Knowing that our faith can shield us from what Satan throws our way, what are some ways you can be prepared for those "fiery darts?

_____

_____

_____

Daily Prayer and Journal Starters

Day 1 – Hebrews 11:1-12:2
Faith has been an essential part of the lives of so many people. This passage shares some powerful examples of believers who lived in and who acted out their faith. Think of examples from your life. Who are the strong examples of faith who have encouraged your walk with the Lord? Consider what kind of faith you are exemplifying. What legacy are you leaving for others?

Day 2 – Philemon 1:4-7
Paul's letter to Philemon expresses his thankfulness for Philemon's faith and for his effectiveness in sharing that faith with others. Thinking of this encouraging letter, write a letter to someone you know. It can be to thank that person for his or her example of faith, or it can be to encourage his or her faith. It can be someone from your past or in your present.

Day 3 – 1 Peter 3:15-16
Ask yourself, "Am I ready?" When someone asks you about your hope, about why you have faith, are you ready to give an answer? This doesn't mean that you are prepared to answer every biblical and theological question, but can you explain why you believe what you believe concerning the Gospel of Christ and your salvation? Spend today's journal entry writing out your story of salvation and what it means to you.

Day 4 – Psalm 96:1-13

Our Lord and Creator is great and worthy to be praised. He is worthy of our uncompromising faith in Him. This chapter repeats the idea of declaring God's greatness to the world. How can you share your faith in the Lord with someone today?

Day 5 – Colossians 3:12-13

Our faith in God revolves around the fact that Christ gave Himself so we could have forgiveness of our sins. Forgiveness and faith go hand in hand. Part of our faith in God is being willing to follow His example and offer forgiveness to those who have wronged us. Is there anyone in your life that you need to forgive?

Day 6 – 1 John 2:1-2

John's letter was written to encourage strength against sin. This letter also reminds us of the powerful role Christ played to give us not only forgiveness of our sins, but to make us as though our sins had not been committed. Christ is our sacrifice, our advocate, our hope, and our life. Describe how this knowledge affects your attitude and faith concerning Jesus and all He has done for you.

Day 7 – Romans 8:1

Christ offers forgiveness and no condemnation to those who are faithful walking according to the Spirit and letting the Spirit direct their lives. Faith in Christ means turning from self and walking toward Christ and His ways. Think of any examples in Scripture or in your life of people who let God lead their lives. Think of other examples that chose self over God for their direction. What difference can you see in the lives they lead?

Deeper Study

Read 2 Peter 1:2-11. It is by inspiration that these words give us all things pertaining to life and godliness. Seeking the promises of God leads us to grow in our faith and to add to it virtues that

will strengthen our walk with Him. Twice in this passage, the idea of "diligence" is presented. Consider that as you examine each quality that we are encouraged to add to our faith. Describe what each of these qualities means to you and how you will need diligence to pursue them.

.... Notes ....

G... Grow in Grace

"Grow in the grace and knowledge of our Lord and Savior Jesus Christ. To Him be the glory both now and forever. Amen."
2 Peter 3:18

Defining Grace: What is it?

Grace is something most of us desire, but few of us could explain to someone else. It is often, and rightly, defined as a free gift. Grace is described as undeserved merit or favor, someone giving you something that you did not work for and you did not deserve because of your own actions or lack thereof. God's grace is much more than this though. This grace is God's life, His power, and His righteousness coming to us, the undeserving and unworthy. It is freely offered to everyone who is willing to accept it.

In the Old Testament, the word for grace is the Hebrew word *Chen* (khane), which means "favor or graciousness." It is the picture of someone in a position of power bending down or stooping in kindness to an inferior. It is a beautiful picture of God's relationship or attitude toward His people. The King coming down to where we are.

In the New Testament, this picture becomes even clearer. The Greek word *Charis* (karis), which is defined as "the divine influence upon the heart and its reflection in the life." The actions of Christ show us God's grace, His divine influence that stepped in the place of death for us and saved our lives. That is grace.

Romans 5:8 tells us, *"But God demonstrates His own love*

toward us, in that while we were still sinners, Christ died for us."
From the introduction of Christ in the New Testament, we realize
that the motivation behind God's grace is love. God loves us and
did everything necessary to show us that love and to enable us to
once again be with Him.

Do We Understand Grace?

When it comes to understanding the power and magnitude
of the grace of God, there are some key things we need to realize.
First, we must recognize how totally undeserving of God's grace
we really are! In Romans 3:23, Paul wrote that we have all sinned
and fall short of God's glory. Like it or not, not one of us is perfect!
We have all at some time in our lives chosen something that was
against God and His commands.

Because of this sin, we were dead in our sins, separated
from God completely. Just as those who are physically dead have
no power to do anything of themselves, so we who are dead in our
sins have absolutely no power to do anything to save ourselves.
We have no hope of doing anything of ourselves to correct that sin
problem. Even at our best, we are so undeserving of God and His
blessings. There are two wonderful words that help us with this,
however, "But God." Look at Ephesians 2:4-5,

*"But God, who is rich in mercy, because of His great love with
which He loved us, even when we were dead in trespasses, made
us alive together with Christ (by grace you have been saved)."*

But God made us alive! Do we grasp how wonderfully
powerful that is?! We were dead and powerless to do anything,
but God, through Jesus, made us alive! That is His grace. We
could do nothing for ourselves to earn this gift. We had nothing in
and of ourselves to offer Him. It was all God!

This leads us to the next key that we need to make sure we
grasp: the generous nature of our God. The breathtaking news for
us is that God loved us so much, He wants us so much, that He
took the necessary steps to overcome what we could not!
Knowing us as He does, knowing what we were going to do even
before He created us, He planned before the foundation of the

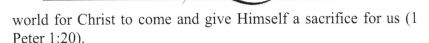

world for Christ to come and give Himself a sacrifice for us (1 Peter 1:20).

Romans 5:6 explains to us, *"For when we were still without strength, in due time Christ died for the ungodly."* While we were powerless, Christ died for us—the ungodly! He didn't have to. He could have left us where we were to pay the price for the sinful choices we made. No, He wanted to! He desired to give of Himself for us, and He gave everything He had for everything we were and are going to be!

Look at what Paul wrote in 2 Corinthians 8:9, *"For you know the grace of our Lord Jesus Christ, that though He was rich, yet for your sakes He became poor, that you through His poverty might become rich."*

He gave up the glories of Heaven to come to earth, to suffer, be humiliated, spat upon, beaten, mocked, and crucified. He did not come in royal robes and riches. He did not receive honor and special treatment. No, He came living a humble, simple life, so that one day we could experience the splendor of heaven with Him! Do We Appreciate It?

What Does Grace Mean for Us?

The grace of God is something to seek after and strive for! It is something to desire for our lives and for the lives of those around us. The Bible tells us of some individuals who found God's grace. Their lives are an example to us as we strive to live ours for the Lord. Were they perfect? No. Were they different? Well, yes and no. No, they were not different from us. They were real humans with real difficulties in their lives. They were humans who were striving to, in most cases, just survive in this world. Yet they were very different from the world around them in which they lived their lives. That difference, that Godly difference, led to them being recognized for who they were, and their stories are recorded forever for us in God's Word.

Noah

Noah lived in a time when the Bible tells us the world was full of corruption. It is recorded in Genesis 6:5, *"...the Lord saw that the wickedness of man was great in the earth, and that every intent of the thoughts of his heart was only evil continually."* Sometimes it seems close to the world we find ourselves in today. Things were so bad, in fact, that in verse 6, it says that God was sorry He had made man, that He was grieved in His heart because of man's wickedness. Mankind was so awful that God was sorry that He had made us. As you read it, you can feel the sorrow in the words.

Yet, Genesis 6:8 tells us that one man, Noah, found grace in the eyes of God. He stood out from those around him by the life he lived. He stood up for his beliefs in God despite his wicked surroundings. Verse 9 says he was a just man, and, most importantly, he walked with God. His life made a statement to all those around him, even if they didn't listen. Noah was recognized for being different from the world around him, and that difference led to the salvation of the human race from the world's destruction.

Moses

Moses also found grace in the eyes of the Lord.

"Yet You have said, 'I know you by name, and you have also found grace in My sight.'" Exodus 33:12b

Moses was not a perfect man. At this point in his life, he had changed from the honored, adopted grandson of the Pharaoh of Egypt to a murderer running for his life, living as a shepherd in the land of Midian, and then to a prophet of the Almighty God called to return to Egypt and free God's people from slavery. Moses had experienced some rough times in his life. But he grew in knowing who he was, and he humbled his life before God.

In verse 16 of that chapter, Moses asked an important question. *"How then will it be known that your people and I have found grace in Your sight, except You God go with us?"* Moses recognized that there was a difference between being from the world and being those who were in God's grace. This difference was shown by being in the presence of God. Moses continued on in verse 16 to say to God, *"So we shall be separate, Your people and I, from all the people who are upon the face of the earth."*

114

From the examples of both Noah and Moses, it seems that part of being in the grace of God is to live a life that is different from the world. We need to be separate, be different, live differently, and do things differently than the people "upon the face of the earth."

How do we use this knowledge in our own lives? When we are surrounded by a world that does not act like it wants anything to do with God, how can we strive to grow in God's grace? Will people today recognize that we are different? Will they see that we have found grace in the eyes of the Lord? How will we be known as His children? Yes. Yes, to all of it. When we act like God's children, then God's grace will set us apart. God's grace will show in our lives. Our obedience to His way of life will be visible to those we come into contact with.

In the book of Acts, we see this played out. We see examples of people who were filled with the grace of God, and we see how it affected those around them. We read of men who went out preaching the Word of God and teaching the people after the death of Stephen. It records that the hand of the Lord was with them and that a great many turned and believed. When it came to the ears of the church in Jerusalem, they sent Barnabas to go and see what was going on.

"When he came and had seen the grace of God, he was glad, and encouraged them all that with purpose of heart they should continue with the Lord." Acts 11:23

The difference in these people was evident to Barnabas. He could see it, and he encouraged them to continue in this different life they were living. Yes, the grace of God will show to those around us, and it can make a difference in their lives as well as ours!

What Does Grace do for Us Personally?

God's grace isn't just some widespread, general concept. It is personal to each one of us, just as it was with the examples of Noah and Moses. As we look further into Exodus 33, we continue to see just how personal this grace was to Moses.

115

"So the Lord said to Moses, "I will also do this thing that you have spoken; for you have found grace in My sight, and I know you by name." Exodus 33:17

Moses wasn't just one of many. He wasn't just considered a child of God, son of Abraham, in the general sense; no, God knew him by name. God knows each one of us personally too. He gives grace to each individual and knows each of our names. But He knows more than just our names; He knows everything about us. David understood how well He was known by God, and He grew strong in that knowledge.

"O Lord, You have searched me and known me. You know my sitting down and my rising up; You understand my thought afar off. You comprehend my path and my lying down, And are acquainted with all my ways. For there is not a word on my tongue, But behold, O Lord, You know it altogether."
Psalm 139:1-4

God's personal knowledge of who we are is important when it comes to His grace. His Word offers us insight into how His grace works in each of our lives, and it teaches us how we can grow in it. Here are several aspects of His grace and what it does for our lives.

Helps Us Stand:
"Therefore, having been justified by faith, we have peace with God through our Lord Jesus Christ, through whom also we have access by faith into this grace in which we stand, and rejoice in hope of the glory of God." Romans 5:1-2

God's grace gives us a sure foundation on which to stand in this world without wavering. We can be assured that, if we are standing in God's grace, we can never be moved!

Justifies Us:
"That having been justified by His grace we should become heirs according to the hope of eternal life." Titus 3:7

His grace makes us justified, or righteous, in His sight and removes the sin that separates us from Him.

Saves Us:
"For the grace of God that brings salvation has appeared to all men." Titus 2:11

God's grace is the reason we have salvation; without it, we could never do enough to make ourselves whole.

Gives Us Power Over Sin:
"For sin shall not have dominion over you, for you are not under law but under grace." Romans 6:14

God's grace gives us the power of Christ in our lives, which says sin and death no longer have dominion over us.

Teaches Us Godliness:
"For the grace of God that brings salvation has appeared to all men, teaching us that, denying ungodliness and worldly lusts, we should live soberly, righteously, and godly in the present age." Titus 2:11-12

Grace shows us what life with God looks like, teaching us to live in that life, obedient and free.

Makes Us What We Are in God:
"For I am the least of the apostles, who am not worthy to be called an apostle, because I persecuted the church of God. But by the grace of God I am what I am, and His grace toward me was not in vain; but I labored more abundantly than they all, yet not I, but the grace of God which was with me." 1 Corinthians 15:9-10

Grace turned Paul from persecutor to preacher, it turns us from sinner to saved.

Empowers Us for Service:

"Through Him we have received grace and apostleship for obedience to the faith among all nations for His name."
Romans 1:5

His grace gives us the tools and ability to serve Him.

Allows Us to Reign:

"For if by the one man's offense death reigned through the one, much more those who receive abundance of grace and of the gift of righteousness will reign in life through the One, Jesus Christ." Romans 5:17

Grace brings us into the family of God as children and co-heirs with Christ. We will reign with Him in the kingdom of God because of His grace!

What Must We do for Grow in Grace?

Believe It: Ephesians 2:8; Romans 5 - Through the foundation of our faith in God, we must believe in the grace He offers and that He offers it all of Himself. It is a gift from our loving Father to His children.

Receive It: Psalm 84:11 – Even though something is offered and given freely, we must still accept it with an open and humble heart. He will give it, and we must receive it. God gives grace and glory. We must realize we are not deserving of His grace; we must not think that we have earned it or that it is owed to us for anything (Romans 4:4). If we could "earn" it, then it would no longer be grace (Romans 11:6). We must not receive it in vain (2 Cor. 6:1), nor must we think that it covers willful disobedience—it does not (Romans 6:1-2, 14).

Continue in It: Acts 13:43 - We must continue to live in God's grace, by His commands, and in His love. We can't accept His wonderful gift and then expect to go back to living by, and in, the ways of the world. We are not to just continue in His grace, but God wants us to abound in it (2 Cor. 8:7).

Use It and Manage It: 1 Peter 4:10; 2 Cor. 9:8 - God gives all of us spiritual gifts and talents to use in His kingdom. As we continue to grow in service to Him, we will find ourselves growing in His grace. He is not only able to sufficiently give us what we need to do our work for Him but graces us abundantly for the work!

Speak It: - Prov. 22:11; Eph. 4:29 - We must speak with grace on our lips and with words that will impart grace to those who hear them.

Spread It: 2 Corinthians 4:15 - Once we have received the grace of God and understand the amazing gift we have, we must take the opportunities to share it with others. We need to show thankfulness for all He has done for us, and we must want others to know the grace of God. When it spreads, the thanksgiving for it will spread as well.

Power Verse

"For the law was given through Moses, but grace and truth
came through Jesus Christ."
John 1:17

G... Grow in Grace

Worksheet

"Grow in the grace and knowledge of our Lord and Savior Jesus Christ. To Him be the glory both now and forever. Amen."
2 Peter 3:18

Defining Grace: What is it?

The Old Testament Hebrew word *Chen* (khane) means

_____

The New Testament Greek word *Charis* (karis) means

_____

"But God demonstrates His own _____ toward us, in that while we were still sinners, Christ died for us." Romans 5:8

What is the motivation behind God's grace? _____

_____

Do We Understand Grace?

According to Romans 3:23, how many of us deserve God's grace? _____

"For _____ have sinned and fall short of the glory of God."

"But God, who is rich in mercy, because of His great love with which He loved us, even when we were _____ in trespasses, made us _____ together with Christ (by grace you have been saved)." Ephesians 2:4-5

What state were we in before God's grace saved us? _____

What were we made together with Christ? _____

Thinking how someone who is dead has no power, what do you think about what Christ has done for each of us? _____

"For when we were still without strength, in due time Christ died for the _____." Romans 5:6

"For you know the grace of our Lord Jesus Christ, that though He was _____, yet for _____ sakes He became _____, that you through His poverty might become rich."
2 Corinthians 8:9

What does this sacrifice mean to you? _____

What Does Grace Mean for Us?

Noah
Read Genesis 6:5. Describe the state of world in Noah's day.

Compare this to the world today. _____

Read Genesis 6:8-9 and describe Noah's character. _____

What about Noah should we try to imitate in our own lives? ___
_____
_____

Moses

Moses was not a perfect man. Describe the life of Moses. _____
_____
_____
_____

What makes him an example of growing in God's grace? _____
_____
_____

Look at Exodus 33:16. What did Moses see as a need for the people that we can still use today? _____
_____
_____

"When he came and had _____ the grace of God, he was glad, and encouraged them all that with purpose of heart they should continue with the Lord." Acts 11:23

When we live differently and live in God's ways, what will the world notice? _____
_____
_____

What Does Grace do for Us Personally?

"So the Lord said to Moses, 'I will also do this thing that you have spoken; for you have found grace in My sight, and I know you by _____.'" Exodus 33:17

How personally does God know you? Consider the verse above as well as Psalm 56:8; Matthew 10:30; and Psalm 139:2. _____

122

_____

_____
_____
_____

"O Lord, You have searched me and known me. You know my _____ _____ and my _____ _____; You understand my thought afar off. You comprehend my path and my lying down, And are acquainted with _____ my ways. For there is not a word on my tongue, But behold, O Lord, You _____ it altogether."Psalm 139:1-4

In your own words, how does the grace of God help us in each of these areas?

Helps Us Stand: Romans 5:1-2 _____

_____
_____

Justifies Us: Titus 3:7 _____

_____
_____

Saves Us: Titus 2:11 _____

_____
_____

Gives Us Power Over Sin: Romans 6:14 _____

_____
_____

Teaches Us Godliness: Titus 2:11-12 _____

_____
_____

Makes Us What We Are in God: 1 Corinthians 15:9-10 _____

_____
_____

Empowers Us for Service: Romans 1:5 _____

_____

_____

Allows Us to Reign: Romans 5:17 _____

_____

_____

What Must We do for Grow in Grace?
Read the given verses and think about the different areas in which we can grow in grace, and give examples from your life of what it would look like. What would change if you grew spiritually in each of these areas?

Believe It: Ephesians 2:8; Romans 5 - _____

_____

_____

Receive It: Psalm 84:11- _____

_____

_____

Continue in It: Acts 13:43 - _____

_____

_____

Use It and Manage It: 1 Peter 4:10; 2 Cor. 9:8 - _____

_____

_____

Speak It: Prov. 22:11; Eph. 4:29 - _____

_____

_____

Spread It: 2 Corinthians 4:15 - _____

_____

_____

Daily Prayer and Journal Starters

Day 1 – Proverbs 22:11 and John 15:14-16
Our grace is most often shown to others by our speech. Proverbs tells us that those who have grace on their lips will be a friend to the King. John records how Jesus said we were His friends if we follow His commandments. Explain how you relate to the idea of showing grace to others in your speech and how that connects with how Jesus asks us to treat others with love.

Day 2 – John 1:14-17
John tells us how Jesus was the full embodiment of both grace and truth. He taught the full truth of God with a grace and kindness that the world did not understand. Thinking of how Christ interacted with people, find one example of Christ's grace, and explain it in your own words. How would it make you feel if you were in that person's shoes?

Day 3 – Romans 15:15 and Hebrews 4:16
Paul stated that he wrote to the church at Rome boldly because of the grace given to Him by God. He recognized the forgiveness He had been given, and he carried the bold desire to share that forgiveness with others. The Hebrew writer reminds us that we can come boldly to the throne of grace. Too often, we are afraid to speak boldly for Christ and to stand up for Him as Paul did. What inhibits you from speaking boldly for Christ? What steps can you take to overcome those inhibitions and speak boldly about the grace you have been given?

Day 4 – 1 Corinthians 15:10
Paul gives all credit to God for him becoming the minister that he was for Christ. He said it was the grace of God that changed

him from a persecutor of the Lord's church to a worker who labored "more abundantly than they all." Think about the ways God's grace has made you the person you are today. Make a list of the areas of your life that His grace has changed you. Read over your list and let it motivate you to be a worker for Him who labors abundantly through His grace.

Day 5 – 2 Corinthians 4:15
Grace is powerful and there is enough for everyone. Write a thank you to God for what His grace has done in your life. Expand that and think about the people you are close to. List the reasons you are thankful for God's grace in their lives as well. Let thanksgiving abound today because of the grace of God.

Day 6 – 2 Corinthians 8:6-8
We cannot forget to grow in grace. Paul writes to the Christians in Corinth that, as they grow and abound in their faith, in their speech, in their knowledge, and in all diligence to strengthen their walk with Christ, they were to abound in grace. We cannot forget grace, to depend on God's grace for strength and to show God's grace to everyone we meet. Write a list of ways you can work to grow in showing God's grace this week.

Day 7 – 2 Corinthians 9:8
God has said that He will supply our every need. Here He states that He will make grace abound toward us so that we will not only have sufficiency in all things (enough of what we need to serve Him) but that we will have an abundance for every good work. Think of ways you can serve God. Look for His grace in supplying you with the abundance you need to succeed in that work. Pray to ask God for success as you work in His kingdom to teach others about Him or to strengthen the brethren around you.

Deeper Study

Read Acts 11:1-18. Paul was given a vision and then sent to the area is Caesarea where he taught the truth of God to the Gentiles there. Think about God's grace as here we see it was opened beyond the Jews to this household and, essentially, to the rest of the world, that all people who believe in God can now receive His grace and the gift of His salvation. God's grace extended beyond the family of Abraham to include you and me. Focus in on verses 17-18. Think about how this gift of life was given to you and reflect on how that makes you feel.

.... Notes ....

H....... Humble yourselves

*"Humble yourselves in the sight of the Lord,
and He will lift you up." James 4:10*

As we read in our main verse above, when we place ourselves correctly before God and humble ourselves, He will lift us up. We all want to feel lifted up, supported, and praised. Who better to be in our cheering section than the Creator of Heaven and Earth! Whose encouragement and support means more than His? The praise of man should never compare with one day hearing the words, *"Well done, good and faithful servant; you were faithful over a few things, I will make you ruler over many things. Enter into the joy of your lord"* (Matthew 25:21).

Sometimes, though, the hard thing is waiting for that. It becomes such a temptation to do things or to act in certain ways to achieve the praise of those around us, to attempt to lift ourselves up instead of waiting for God's timing.

1 Peter 5:6 tells us He will lift us up in due time!

*"Therefore, humble yourselves under the mighty hand of God,
that He may exalt you in due time."*

God has a plan for us, He needs for us to trust Him and wait humbly for it to come to fruition. He will raise us up to the place He wants us to be, but the timing of that is for Him to

choose. We cannot place ourselves in positions we have no power to be in.

In this lesson, though we will learn what it means to be truly humble, see examples of those who chose humility in their lives, and witness the outcomes of those who did not. We will see the power that being humble actually gives us and the true place it puts us in. All of this leads us on a journey to strengthen our own spiritual lives and to draw us closer to our God, who desires to see us succeed in Him.

Humility in Example

There are so many people in the Bible who offer us examples of living a humble life before God, people who have faced power and poverty and have overcome every obstacle with humility. God wants us to learn from these people!

Moses: The Most Humble Man on Earth

"Now the man Moses was very humble, more than all men who were on the face of the earth." Numbers 12:3

I have heard it said that to truly test a person's ability to be a great leader, don't just give him responsibilities—as many can rise to that occasion—but give him privilege and see how he handles it. See what he does with the power and the way he treats those people who are now in his charge. Moses was given that privilege.

Moses was raised in Pharaoh's palace with all the privilege of royalty. He gave that away to eventually lead a people who were disrespectful and complaining. (Read Hebrews 11:23-29). He was a leader to thousands, hundreds of thousands of people. To the world, a position like this is sought as the power to lord over and rule. Moses did not see it as such.

After an occasion of much complaining from the people, Moses turns to God, complaining himself of the situation, but asking for help in the best possible place. He is worn down and exhausted from his role as leader, and God instructs him to choose seventy men whom God will give His spirit, and they can help Moses with the task of caring for these people. (Read Numbers

11:24-29). While Moses was pleased with what the Lord was doing to ease his burden of caring for such a large multitude, Joshua didn't handle it as well. It is easy to see the difference in attitude between Moses and Joshua. Although well-meaning, it was still hard for Joshua to see, with the humility of Moses, that others being given the spirit of God was a blessing and was not taking anything away from the blessings God had for Moses.

Jesus: The Humbled and Exalted Christ

"Let this mind be in you which was also in Christ Jesus, who, being in the form of God, did not consider it robbery to be equal with God, but made Himself of no reputation, taking the form of a bondservant, and coming in the likeness of men. And being found in appearance as a man, He humbled Himself and became obedient to the point of death, even the death of the cross. Therefore God also has highly exalted Him and given Him the name which is above every name, that at the name of Jesus every knee should bow, of those in heaven, and of those on earth, and of those under the earth, and that every tongue should confess that Jesus Christ is Lord, to the glory of God the Father."
Philippians 2:5-11

Jesus is part of the Godhead, Creator of Heaven and Earth, yet He came to earth and took on the form of a servant, learning humility and obedience. He took on the role of Son to the Father to teach us humility. His example is one we must pay close attention to.

During His life, everything Jesus said and did was not of Himself, but of the Father's will. He often said, "Not My will but Yours." He came, not to exalt Himself, but to fulfill what God desired. He never lifted Himself up but raised the Father to glory.

John 5:30 records Jesus saying, *"I can of Myself do nothing. As I hear, I judge; and My judgment is righteous, because I do not seek My own will but the will of the Father who sent Me."* This is the truest example of humility that we can have, learning not to seek our own will, but the will of our God in heaven.

Paul's Example

"And when they had come to him, he said to them: 'You know, from the first day that I came to Asia, in what manner I always lived among you, serving the Lord with all humility, with many tears and trials which happened to me by the plotting of the Jews.'" Acts 20:18-19

Although some people seem to be naturally more humble than others, there are some who need a reminder of who God really is to change their ways. After his experience coming face-to-face with the Lord, Paul's whole life changed. The way he conducted himself changed from someone who held the coats of the men who stoned Stephen to a humble servant of God.

Paul's attitude changed from an up-and-coming Jewish leader, wealthy, son of a Pharisee, and set to be trained by one of the best teachers to a man who willingly gave all of that up and counted it as rubbish. This was because he learned the truth of Christ and what really mattered in life. (Read Philippians 3:7-11). His whole life changed, and he learned humility.

"And I thank Christ Jesus our Lord who has enabled me, because He counted me faithful, putting me into the ministry, although I was formerly a blasphemer, a persecutor, and an insolent man; but I obtained mercy because I did it ignorantly in unbelief. And the grace of our Lord was exceedingly abundant, with faith and love which are in Christ Jesus. This is a faithful saying and worthy of all acceptance, that Christ Jesus came into the world to save sinners, of whom I am chief."
1 Timothy 1:12-15

Paul shows us that people can change. God wants us to change. He knows that we are a sinful people, but He knows us deeper and knows what we are capable of through Him. In Colossians 3:12, we are given the characteristics of a new woman in Christ, the elect of God; listed among all those qualities that we should desire to have in our lives is humility.

Other Lives and Outcomes That Changed

God doesn't want anyone to perish; He wants all to come to Him (2 Peter 3:9), but it must be on His terms, and He requires humility from those who serve Him. There are many examples in Scripture of people who were in need of a change of heart, in need of God's patience and of opportunities that were offered and accepted. These examples should give any of us hope that God isn't finished with us just because we mess up and get on the wrong path. No, God's forgiveness is available, and these examples show us that a change of outcome is possible from what could have been a disaster. Read each text and think of how these lives changed.

- **Ahab** – 1 Kings 21:28-29 – Eventually humbled himself before God, and God did not send calamity during his days, not until the days of Ahab's son.
- **Israelite People** – Leviticus 26:40-42 - So many times they were humbled and had to change their complaining ways, yet they were still God's chosen people, and He did not give up on them.
- **Josiah** – 2 Kings 22:18-20 (and recounted again in 2 Chron. 34:23-28) - Realized what the people had lost and been guilty of and tore his clothes and wept in God's presence and saved the people.
- **God's People** – 2 Chron. 7:12-14 - God speaking to Solomon after the dedication of the temple on what a change of heart will do!
- **Hezekiah** – 2 Chron. 32:24-26 - Prayed to God for help, but then was too proud to truly accept what he was receiving. God had to humble him, but he changed!
- **Manasseh** – 2 Chron. 33:9-13, 18-20 - He took a lot of convincing! He was dragged around by a hook through the nose, but his heart was changed! Sometimes it takes something big to get our attention.
- **Nebuchadnezzar** – Dan. 4:28-37 - After his pride, God humbled him to graze as a beast of the field to show him the True Lord!

133

Repeatedly through the book of Isaiah, he tells that the people will be humbled because of their sin. (Is. 2:11-12; 5:14-16; and 10:33-34 to name a few). But one of the wonderful things about God is that it doesn't end there. He also speaks of their recovery when they chose to return to God as a humble people. (Is. 29: 17-19). God wants us all to come to Him, and when we do, He will not turn us away.

Those Who Refused to Change

For as many examples as there are of people who accepted God's grace and changed, there are as many of those who chose not to, who hardened their hearts and refused to bow to the Lord. The outcome for these people is not pleasant. God will save the humble people, but the haughty He will bring down. (2 Sam. 22:28)

- **Zedekiah** – 2 Chron. 36:11-16 - Refused to humble himself before God. Jerusalem was destroyed with no compassion vs. 17-20
- **Pharaoh** – Exodus 10:3 - Hardened his heart. God sent the Ten Plagues on Egypt, his country was destroyed, and many suffered death because of his pride.
- **Amon** – 2 Chron. 33:22-24 - Unlike his father, Manasseh, he didn't humble himself, but increased in his guilt. He ended up being killed by Servants – Vs. 25.
- **Judah** – Jeremiah 44:7-10 - Worshiped idols and didn't show reverence to the one, true God! Sadly, God sets His face against them – vs. 11.
- **Belshazzar** – Daniel 5:22 - Even knowing all that happened to Nebuchadnezzar, and with the writing on the wall, he refused to change and was killed - vs. 26-30.

God's Desire for Us

"Therefore whoever humbles himself as this little child is the greatest in the kingdom of heaven." Matthew 18:4

Pride is not a quality you tend to see in children, not the

way it is abused as adults. God desires for us to have the humble attitudes of children, who, though proud of themselves and their accomplishments, do not use it in a way that is harmful to those around them. Children simply gain the pleasure of a job done well.

Imagine a small child seeing Mom place a just finished work of art on the refrigerator. There is a huge smile, the feeling of appreciation and love, but nothing dangerous or harmful. A child is pure and hopeful, dependent on others, sweet and innocent to everyone around him. We are to have that same type of personality, that joy in everything around us, that desire for everyone to succeed, and that dependence upon God, pure and complete as a child's upon his parent.

How to Learn Humility?

For many of us, humility, that true childlike humility, must be learned. But how? Where do we learn how to be humble like those examples who changed their lives to become humble servants of God? If this is an area where we struggle in our spiritual walk, how do we grow stronger in humility? It seems like a hard area to grow in, yet there are ways God helps us to learn humility, but they aren't always easy.

- **Tests and Trials of Life** – Deut. 8:2-3, 16 - Israelites were made to wander for 40 years to humble them. Their pride and grumbling took a while to overcome. Often it is the hardships of our life, the struggles, that will bring us to our knees in humility before God, making us realize we can't do this alone! When things seem to be going well is when pride builds, and we look at all we have done, but it is in the difficult moments when we really see how much we need God. We must learn to keep that attitude when the trials are over.
- **Prayers for Humility** – Ezra 8:21-23 - God will help us if we just ask Him! He wants us to place our dependence upon Him. He wants us to look to Him. He has the power and strength to help us, and He will never tire or grow weary. We must learn to turn to Him and trust Him.
- **Choice** – Daniel 10:12 - Humility is an attitude, the right

135

attitude, and as usual, it is a matter of choosing this attitude over one of pride. It is a choice found in moments when we would like to lift ourselves for the recognition of others—we need to remember that we must let God do the lifting!

- **Associating Ourselves with Humble People** – Romans 12:15-16 - We reflect those whom we spend the most time with. If we desire to have a humble attitude, we will learn it most from spending time with those who show it regularly. Who we associate with matters. If we are surrounded by prideful people, it will be harder to reflect a spirit of humility.
- **Looking Out for the Interest of Others** – Phil. 2:3-4 - When we are placing the needs of others over our own wants and desires, we will learn humility! By submitting to one another (1 Peter 5:5-6) and being no respecter of persons, but showing humility to all people (Titus 3:1-2), we will grow in the humble attitude God desires for us. We will find our focus to be less on ourselves.
- **Strive to Imitate Jesus** – Phil. 2:5-8 - Our ultimate example of humility and service! God and Creator of the world coming to earth to serve us and show us how to serve others! John 13:1-17 shows us the powerful example of Jesus lowering Himself to the lowest position of the house and washing the disciple's feet! What a powerful lesson for all those present, and it is still teaching us today.
- **Submit Self to God** – James 4:6-7 - We are our own worst enemy; this is true in so many aspects of our lives. But when we can learn to get over ourselves, trust in God, and submit our will to His, we will learn humility. We must have the attitude of John the Baptizer, "*He must increase, but I must decrease*" (John 3:30).
- **Seek It** – Zeph. 2:3 – If we are to grow in and have humility in our lives, as part of who we are, then we must want it; we must seek it. We must seek out opportunities to practice it and strive to encourage it in our lives and in the lives of those around us. Just like growing our physical muscles, it requires work and practice to grow in our

136

desire for humility.

Encouraging Psalms and Proverbs Concerning Humility

There is so much in Scripture to encourage us as we strive to grow in the qualities God wants for us, including humility. As you are seeking to grow in this area and learn more about the way God views the humble, take time to read these Scriptures. Look at not only what they mean for your own life, but what they teach us about God and who He is.

- God does not forget the cry of the humble - Psalm 9:12
- God saves the humble - Psalm 18:27
- God guides the humble and teaches them His way - Psalm 25:9
- God lifts up the humble - Psalm 147:6
- God beautifies the humble with salvation - Psalm 149:4
- God gives grace to the humble - Proverbs 3:34
- Pride brings shame, but humility brings wisdom - Proverbs 11:2
- Better to be counted with the humble than with the proud - Proverbs 16:19
- The humble will retain honor - Proverbs 29:23
- He who humbles himself will be exalted - Matt. 23:11-12; Luke 14:10-11; 18:13-14

Power Verse

"By humility and the fear of the Lord
are riches and honor and life."
Proverbs 22:4

H....... Humble

Yourselves

Worksheet

*"Humble yourselves in the sight of the Lord,
and He will lift you up." James 4:10*

When you read these words of Jesus, what comes to your mind?
*"Well done, good and faithful servant; you were faithful over a
few things, I will make you ruler over many things. Enter into the
joy of your lord." Matthew 25:21.*

_____

_____

_____

*"Therefore, humble yourselves under the mighty hand of God,
that He may _____ you in _____ _____." 1 Peter 5:6*

Waiting if often hard for us to handle. God says He will lift us up
in His time. Is waiting on God difficult for you? Why?

_____

_____

_____

Humility in Example

Who was known as the most humble man on earth? _____

What are some qualities in the life of Moses that you most admire?

_____

_____

_____

Read Hebrews 11:23-29. What feelings does this short summary of the life of Moses bring to mind? What stands out to you?

_____

_____

_____

_____

Read Numbers 11:24-29. God does not want us to do things alone. Think of some of the people God has placed in your life and how do they help you?

_____

_____

_____

Jesus: The Humbled and Exalted Christ – Philippians 2:5-11
Jesus is the ultimate example of humility. Describe an event in His life that shows this to you the most.

_____

_____

_____

"I can of Myself do _____. As I hear, I judge; and My judgment is righteous, because I do not seek My own will but the will of the _____ who sent Me." John 5:30

Paul's Example - Acts 20:18-19
How did Paul's life change after his encounter with Jesus?

_____

_____

_____

"This is a faithful saying and worthy of all acceptance, that

139

Christ Jesus came into the world to save sinners, of whom I am
_____ *.” 1 Timothy 1:15*

How has your life changed since coming to know Jesus?

_____

_____

_____

Other Lives and Outcomes That Changed
List something that stood out the most to you about the following people in Scripture.

- **Ahab** – 1 Kings 21:28-29 – _____

  _____

- **Israelite People** – Leviticus 26:40-42 - _____

  _____

- **Josiah** – 2 Kings 22:18-20 - _____

  _____

- **God's People** – 2 Chron. 7:12-14 - _____

  _____

- **Hezekiah** – 2 Chron. 32:24-26 - _____

  _____

- **Manasseh** – 2 Chron. 33:9-13, 18-20 - _____

  _____

- **Nebuchadnezzar** – Dan. 4: 28-37 - _____

  _____

  _____

Those Who Refused to Change
What is a lesson you learned from all of the following people who refused to humble themselves before God?

- **Zedekiah** – 2 Chron. 36:11-16 - _____

  _____

- **Pharaoh** – Exodus 10:3 - _____

  _____

- **Amon** – 2 Chron. 33:22-24 - _____

  _____

- **Judah** – Jeremiah 44:7-10 - _____

  _____

- **Belshazzar** – Daniel 5:22 - _____

  _____

God's Desire for Us

"Therefore whoever _____ himself as this little child is the _____ in the kingdom of heaven." Matthew 18:4

What does it mean to you to humble yourself as a little child?

_____

_____

_____

How to Learn Humility?

Tests and Trials of Life – Deut. 8:2-3, 16 – How would a humble spirit, compared to a prideful spirit, change how you handle trials in your life?

_____

_____

_____

Prayers for Humility – Ezra 8:21-23 – What areas would you pray for God to help you be more humble in?

_____

141

Choice – Daniel 10:12 – How do your choices affect your attitude?

Associating Ourselves with Humble People – Romans 12:15-16 – Think of the people you are around daily. How are their attitudes affecting   your   own?

Looking Out for the Interest of Others – Phil. 2:3-4 – In what ways could you practice putting others needs ahead of your own?

Strive to Imitate Jesus – Phil. 2:5-8 – What area of Jesus' life would you most like to emulate to grow in humility?

Submit Self to God – James 4:6-7 – John said, *"He must* _____*, but I must* _____*." John 3:30.* What areas of your life do you think you need to decrease in in order to grow in Christ-like humility?

Seek It – Zeph. 2:3 – What opportunities could be around you, where you could strive to grow in your humility and overcome pride?

_____

_____

_____

Encouraging Psalms and Proverbs Concerning Humility
Consider the following verses about humility and God. Record your thoughts and reflect on what they teach you about how your attitude of humility, versus pride, affects your relationship with God.

- God does not forget the cry of the humble - Psalm 9:12
- God saves the humble - Psalm 18:27
- God guides the humble and teaches them His way - Psalm 25:9
- God lifts up the humble - Psalm 147:6
- God beautifies the humble with salvation - Psalm 149:4
- God gives grace to the humble - Proverbs 3:34
- Pride brings shame, but humility brings wisdom - Proverbs 11:2
- Better to be counted with the humble than with the proud - Proverbs 16:19
- The humble will retain honor - Proverbs 29:23
- He who humbles himself will be exalted - Matt. 23:11-12; Luke 14:10-11; 18:13-14

_____

_____

_____

_____

_____

_____

_____

_____

_____

_____

_____

Daily Prayer and Journal Starters

Day 1 – Colossians 2:18-23
Read this passage carefully and think of the differences in character between those with true humility and false humility. Which type of person would you rather be and be around?

Day 2 – Psalm 10:17
David wrote that God will hear the desires of the humble and prepare their hearts. What are your desires? What preparation does your heart need for God to work in it?

Day 3 – Psalm 34:2; 69:30-32
In both passages, the humble is said to rejoice over others praising God. Describe how a having a humble heart would change how you view other's accomplishments? How does having a humble heart change how you would view others who are facing hard times?

Day 4 – Isaiah 57:15
Isaiah records God saying that He will dwell with and revive those with a contrite and humble heart. Sometimes we need reviving in heart and spirit. How would you ask God to revive your spirit? In what areas do you feel the need to be revived?

Day 5 – Acts 20:17-24
Paul noted that he served the Lord with humility, knowing from the Spirit what awaited him. Our attitude toward God and the future He has in mind for us matters. How we serve Him, approach His throne, and go about following His commands must be with humility of spirit. Reflect on Paul's life, and what humility looked like in his life.

Day 6 – Romans 12:16

We are reminded here of two things: what we think matters, and who we spend time with matters. We are to be humble and to associate (watch who influences our lives) with those who are humble. This is relevant to those of all ages. Consider who you spend the most time with and the influence they have on your behavior. Do your personality and attitude change in different crowds? How do the attitudes of those around you affect your own?

Day 7 – Proverbs 22:4

What the world views as riches and what God views as riches are very different. The riches of God come with humility and godly fear. Describe the riches, honor, and life that God has for each of us when we serve Him with humility and fear.

Deeper Study

Read Jeremiah 13:18 and Job 40:11. Jeremiah recorded words to warn the king and queen of their pride. Job prayed that God would humble everyone who is proud. Being in a position of power is not a reason to have an attitude of pride. Instead, it is an opportunity to serve those around you. God's qualification for leadership positions has always been based on service, not merit. Think of David being chosen as king (1 Samuel 16:1-13) and how differently God saw him from how mankind saw him. What qualities did David have? What qualities should we have in leadership roles? How much difference would it make if our leaders showed more humility?

.... Notes ....

I...... Inheritance: Daughters of the King

"Blessed be the God and Father of our Lord Jesus Christ, who according to His abundant mercy has begotten us again to a living hope through the resurrection of Jesus Christ from the dead, to an inheritance incorruptible and undefiled and that does not fade away, reserved in heaven for you." 1 Peter 1:3-4

Family is important. Where we come from is vital to knowing who we are and where we are going. Jesus knew this. John 13:3 tells us, *"Jesus, knowing that the Father had given all things into His hands, and that He had come from God and was going to God..."* It is important for us to also know where we come from (God) and where we are going (back to God) because knowing this directs how we feel about ourselves and the actions we take.

The beautiful truth is that when we are baptized into Christ, washed in His blood, we become part of His family, part of His church, and the children of the Most High God, Creator of the Universe. We are forever changed and are once again part of the royal family of God. A child of the Creator of heaven and earth, co-heir with Christ.

"The Spirit Himself bears witness with our spirit that we are children of God, and if children, then heirs—heirs of God and joint heirs with Christ, if indeed we suffer with Him, that we may also be glorified together." Romans 8:16-17

That would look impressive on a resume, right? I would think that one credential would be enough to say that you were qualified as royalty!

Being the daughter of the King is a blessed gift, yet it is one we don't really appreciate. We don't exactly understand the fullness of what being a child of the King really entails, what it really means for our lives regarding the expectations for how we are to live, as well as the glory of our inheritance.

We don't understand the importance and power of being able to declare to the world

"I AM A DAUGHTER OF THE KING!"

In Galatians 3:26, we read, *"For you are all sons of God through faith in Christ Jesus."* For our purposes here, let me paraphrase it slightly, *"For you are all 'daughters' of God through faith in Christ Jesus."*

Look further into the next few verses; it is our faithful obedience in baptism that makes us the children, the daughters, of the King.

"For you are all sons of God through faith in Christ Jesus. For as many of you as were baptized into Christ have put on Christ. There is neither Jew nor Greek, there is neither slave nor free, there is neither male nor female; for you are all one in Christ Jesus. And if you are Christ's, then you are Abraham's seed, and heirs according to the promise." Galatians 3:26-29

This is something so incredibly special. There is something special about being Daddy's little girl, especially to our

148

heavenly Father. In the book of Zephaniah, God speaks to the children of Israel as though speaking to a daughter,

"Sing, O daughter of Zion!
Shout, O Israel!
Be glad and rejoice with all your heart,
O daughter of Jerusalem!
The Lord your God in your midst,
The Mighty One, will save;
He will rejoice over you with gladness,
He will quiet you with His love,
He will rejoice over you with singing."
Zephaniah 3:14, 17

Doesn't this sound like a doting father? When we know how our loving Father treats His daughters, we realize how precious we are in His sight. Look at the language used here. Look again at verse 17. Doesn't this sound like the words and actions of a Father totally in love with His daughter?

He rejoices over us with gladness – God is happy for us to be in His presence. He wants to spend time with us. He wants us to get to know Him as deeply and closely as He knows each of us.

He quiets us with His love – God desires to calm us when we are hurt, upset, and discouraged. His love is to be a source of strength and peace for our lives. He wants us to turn to Him when we have problems and to trust Him while solving and enduring those problems.

He rejoices over us with singing – God is singing His blessings and love over us! Oh, how we long to feel loved in this world. We reach out and long for it; all the while, God is offering us more love than we can imagine because we are His daughters.

The true princess sparkles in the love and glory of Her Father!

Imitate the Father

How wonderful to have a Father that loves us so, that speaks of us and thinks so highly of us, who knows us so well and makes us sparkle and shine, even when we do not act deserving of that kind of devotion.

We can change that! We can be the daughters He wants us to be; we can behave as He wants His dear children to behave. We just need to know what it means to be His child, to act like His child, to think like His child, to live like His child, and to share in the inheritance as His child.

There are certain truths that come with being a daughter of the King. The first important truth for us to grasp is that we were created in the very image of our Father, in His wonderful likeness.

Being made in the likeness of our Father is not that hard a concept to grasp. My husband and I have three kids. Our youngest, the only girl, is often told that she looks just like her mom. She has taken it so far now that she has started calling herself "mini-mom."

It is flattering to know that she looks up to me and wants to be like me; but it is also a little scary, knowing that she is like me and, more than that, wants to "BE" like me. She watches my every move, hears my every word, and wants to be my little mimic. It makes me very aware of how I act when I see or hear something that I have done come from this little person.

Our Father in Heaven wants that kind of attention from us. We were made in His likeness, with eternal souls, with hearts that can love, with a desire to be in a relationship, with minds that can reason, and with free will to act using all those things He has given us.

The blessed part is, we can act like Him. We can imitate Him and follow His example. We never have to worry about Him having a bad moment or setting a wrong example. He will never

demonstrate something that shouldn't be done. He is the perfect example for us to follow.

Me, I lose my temper; I may get frustrated and short with my kids, or forget to do something for them. I may let them down or hurt their feelings because of my own shortcomings, but none of these things can be true with God!

Ephesians 5:1 tells us that we are to, *"Be imitators of God as dear children."* The Holy Spirit knows what children do; they imitate their parents. We can see it time and time again in the world we live in, and that is what we are called to do, imitate our Father! By imitating the Father, we will grow in our spiritual lives and become closer to Him.

And when we imitate the Father, the world will take notice! As God's children, daughters of the King, princesses, in fact, we need to live a way that the world sees us, knows we are different and can recognize us as one of God's kids!

Daughters of the King Live Differently

When we are imitating the Father, it requires us to live differently from the world around us. God requires something different from His children. We are to put off the old man (old woman) of sin and be renewed in God's ways. Ephesians 4:20-24 tells us,

"But you have not so learned Christ, if indeed you have heard Him and have been taught by Him, as the truth is in Jesus: that you put off, concerning your former conduct, the old man which grows corrupt according to the deceitful lusts, and be renewed in the spirit of your mind, and that you put on the new man which was created according to God, in true righteousness and holiness."

We are taught the truth of God through Jesus (verse 21), and we put on the new man, or rather in our case, the "new woman" created according to God. In what? Created according to

God in Righteousness and Holiness so that we could be like the Father! That is what He wants from us to day-by-day grow in our faith, in our walk, in our spiritual lives, in the example of His Son, and in righteousness and holiness, just like our Father! We are to live a life that looks like the Father, not a life that looks like the world.

We are to bear that image of our Father in Heaven, not just because we are told to, although that should be sufficient, but there is a deeper reason why. In Leviticus 11:44-45, God says,

"For I am the LORD your God. You shall therefore consecrate yourselves, and you shall be holy; for I am holy. Neither shall you defile yourselves with any creeping thing that creeps on the earth. For I am the LORD who brings you up out of the land of Egypt, to be your God. You shall therefore be holy, for I am holy."

The same God who wanted the children of Israel to be separate from the dark world around them, wants us to stand out in this world because He wants us to be like He is, Holy! We are called to live that life different from the world for a purpose.

We are called to live it out in our…

Speech – Col. 4:6 says, *"Let your speech always be with grace, seasoned with salt, that you may know how you ought to answer each one."* As true princesses, we are called to have a different way of speaking, to speak with grace, lifting up those around us. Being daughters of the King means that we must speak as the King speaks. It means that everyone we come into contact with is someone the King loves, even if they don't love Him back, and we must treat them as the King would treat them, including how we speak to them.

Appearance – 1 Peter 3:3-4 says, *"Do not let your adornment be merely outward—arranging the hair, wearing gold, or putting on fine apparel— rather let it be the hidden person of the heart, with*

152

the incorruptible beauty of a gentle and quiet spirit, which is very precious in the sight of God." We are to have the appearance of our Father, to show people a gentle and quiet spirit. That is what our Father finds precious. He does not care what brand of clothing we wear or how we style our hair; He cares about how we carry ourselves since we are bearing His name to the world.

In 1 Peter 5:5-7, we are also called to be clothed in humility. *"Likewise you younger people, submit yourselves to your elders. Yes, all of you be submissive to one another, and be clothed with humility, for "God resists the proud, But gives grace to the humble. Therefore humble yourselves under the mighty hand of God, that He may exalt you in due time, casting all your care upon Him, for He cares for you."* Isn't that last thought nice for us to know and take to heart, that He cares for us! We all want to be cared for, and the Creator of the Universe does just that! When we clothe ourselves in humility and allow God to be God— not only of the universe but of our lives—then we are clothed the way the Father would have us to be.

Attitude - Phil. 2:5 says, *"Let this mind be in you which was also in Christ Jesus."* We are to have the same mind, the same attitude as Christ, the one God sent to save us, to show us the way back to Him! An attitude that knows and follows the greatest commandments: loving God, our Father, with everything we are and loving our neighbor as ourselves.

When we can try each day to do these things, people will see God in us, and they will see and glorify our Father! When we live each day in these ways, we will find ourselves growing in our spiritual lives as we put what the Father wants from us into practice.

Inheritance: Our Father's Promise

There is a reason that this different way of life is so important: the promise of an unfailing Father in heaven! If we live as He commands, then we can be assured that God is faithful in

His promises to us, His daughters and heirs. But what did He promise?

He has promised us Life!

"And this is the promise that He has promised us—eternal life."
1 John 2:25

As we struggle through this life, we must remember that we are not simply going through the motions. We are not just here, living day-to-day with problems and frustrations, and God doesn't see what we are going through. No, He is with us each step of the way. He has promised us eternal life when we endure through it, clinging tightly to Him, our Father!

God has promised us that on the other side of this life, there is life eternal—life without pain, without tears and fears, life where we are with the Father and at peace. But life with Him is not all He has promised as our inheritance as His children. He has promised us the gift of the Holy Spirit, who dwells in us to help us in this life.

"Then Peter said to them, 'Repent, and let every one of you be baptized in the name of Jesus Christ for the remission of sins; and you shall receive the gift of the Holy Spirit. For the promise is to you and to your children, and to all who are afar off, as many as the Lord our God will call.'"
Acts 2:38-39

God has promised us a Helper, someone to be there with us, within us, someone to carry us through and even help us pray when we don't know what to say (Romans 8:26).

"And I will pray the Father, and He will give you another Helper, that He may abide with you forever."
John 14:16

154

God has promised that we shall be heirs to His kingdom along with Jesus. As joint heirs to the kingdom, if we suffer for Christ's sake, He has also promised we will be glorified with Him.

"...and if children, then heirs—heirs of God and joint heirs with Christ, if indeed we suffer with Him, that we may also be glorified together"
Romans 8:17

The Father has promised us, as heirs, a home with Him and an inheritance forever with Him, the Son, and the Spirit. This is the home Jesus went to prepare and promised to come and bring us back to.

"In My Father's house are many mansions; if it were not so, I would have told you. I go to prepare a place for you. And if I go and prepare a place for you, I will come again and receive you to Myself; that where I am, there you may be also."
John 14:2-3

God has promised us a home with Him! What a beautiful thought as His children, a home forever with the Father. Not everyone on this earth is blessed with a home with their earthly Father. God feels our pain; He knows how needed that is for so many. What a beautiful promise that we can have.

"Jesus answered and said to him, "If anyone loves Me, he will keep My word; and My Father will love him, and We will come to him and make Our home with him."
John 14:23

God promised to make a home for His children. He wants to have a home with His children. And a princess trusts in the promises of her King!

A Crown for His Princess!

Our King, our Father, has also promised us a crown. What better promise for a princess, heir to the King? It is a prize to be won for our faithfulness, for living our life of purpose in His image, a sign of our relationship with our Father.

"And everyone who competes for the prize is temperate in all things. Now they do it to obtain a perishable crown, but we for an imperishable crown."
1 Corinthians 9:25

As we live for our King, we are not striving for earthly riches or royalty in earthly kingdoms, but to grow in our spiritual lives for our Heavenly crown. Our glorious treasure in His kingdom, where nothing can take it from us or destroy it.

"...and when the Chief Shepherd appears, you will receive the crown of glory that does not fade away."
1 Peter 5:4

Pay close attention to that verse. It does not say you "might" receive a crown or "maybe if there are any left." We are promised that when He returns, we WILL receive a crown of glory in His kingdom. It's not just for a few, or whoever gets there first, but a crown for all of God's children! The crown is part of our inheritance from the Father.

"I have fought the good fight, I have finished the race, I have kept the faith. Finally, there is laid up for me the crown of righteousness, which the Lord, the righteous Judge, will give to me on that Day, and not to me only but also to all who have loved His appearing."
2 Timothy 4:7-8

And why does He offer us a crown? Because we are His crown, His treasure, and we are precious to Him!

*"For what is our hope, or joy, or crown of rejoicing? Is it not
even you in the presence of our Lord Jesus Christ at His
coming? For you are our glory and joy."*
1 Thessalonians 2:19-20

A princess is the crown jewel of the King!

With the promise of a crown is the promise of a kingdom,
the kingdom we are promised as an inheritance from our Father.
We cannot imagine the splendor of where we are going. The
majesty of the home of our heavenly Father, which He has
promised to us, is beyond what we can see in our mind's eye, but
we can know that living for Him here will be More than worth it!
We can trust that striving every day to grow in our spiritual lives
will have rewards beyond our wildest dreams.

*"No eye has seen, no ear has heard, and no mind has imagined
what God has prepared for those who love him."*
1 Corinthians 2:9 NLT

Power Verse

*"And whatever you do, do it heartily, as to the Lord and not to
men, knowing that from the Lord you will receive the reward of
the inheritance; for you serve the Lord Christ."*
Colossians 3:23-24

I...... Inheritance: Daughters of the King

Worksheet

"Blessed be the God and Father of our Lord Jesus Christ, who according to His abundant mercy has begotten us again to a living hope through the resurrection of Jesus Christ from the dead, to an inheritance incorruptible and undefiled and that does not fade away, reserved in heaven for you." 1 Peter 1:3-4

What does family mean to you? _____
_____
_____

"Jesus, knowing that the Father had given all things into His hands, and that He had come _____ God and was _____ to God." John 13:3

How does knowing that you are a child of God affect how you see yourself?___ _____
_____
_____

"The Spirit Himself bears witness with our spirit that _____ _____ _____ ____ _____, and if children, then heirs—heirs of God and joint heirs with Christ, if indeed we suffer with Him, that we may also be glorified together."
Romans 8:16-17

"I AM A DAUGHTER OF THE KING!"

Personalize Galatians 3:26.

_____

_____

_____

"For you are all sons of God through faith in Christ Jesus. For as many of you as were baptized into Christ have put on Christ. There is neither Jew nor Greek, there is neither slave nor free, there is neither male nor female; for you are all one in Christ Jesus. And if you are Christ's, then you are Abraham's seed, and _____ according to the promise." Galatians 3:26-29

What does being an heir mean? _____

_____

_____

"Sing, O _____ of Zion!
Shout, O Israel!
Be glad and rejoice with all your heart,
O _____ of Jerusalem!
The Lord your God in your midst,
The Mighty One, will save;
He will _____ over you with gladness,
He will _____ you with His love,
He will rejoice over you with _____."
Zephaniah 3:14, 17

What feeling do you have reading the above verses? _____

_____

_____

159

What are the ways the Father loves His daughters?

_____

_____

_____

The true princess sparkles in the love and glory of Her Father!

Imitate the Father

Imitation is only possible if you are paying close attention. How much attention are you giving God? What attributes of God would you most like to imitate in life? _____

_____

_____

> *"Be _____ of God as dear _____."*
> *Ephesians 5:1*

Daughters of the King Live Differently

> *"...and that you put on the new man which was created according to God, in true _____ and _____."*
> *Ephesians 4:24*

> *"You shall therefore be _____, for I am _____."*
> *Leviticus 11:45b*

Define Holy. _____

_____

How can you imitate God in the following ways?
Speech – Col. 4:6 - _____

_____

_____

Appearance – 1 Peter 3:3-4; 1 Peter 5:5-7 - _____

_____

_____

Attitude - Phil. 2:5 - _____

_____

_____

Inheritance: Our Father's Promise

What has God promised for you, His daughter? _____

_____

_____

He has promised us life!

"And this is the promise that He has promised us — _____
_____*."*
1 John 2:25

"Then Peter said to them, 'Repent, and let every one of you be baptized in the name of Jesus Christ for the remission of sins; and you shall receive the _____ *of the Holy Spirit. For the promise is to you and to your children, and to all who are afar off, as many as the Lord our God will call.'"*
Acts 2:38-39

"And I will pray the Father, and He will give you another _____*, that He may abide with you forever."*
John 14:16

Read Romans 8:26. The Spirit helps us in our darkest times. How has the Spirit been there for you in your life? _____

_____

_____

"In My Father's house are many mansions; if it were not so, I would have told you. I go to prepare a place for you. And if I go and _____ ___ _____ _____ _____, I will come again and receive you to Myself; that where I am, there you may be also." John 14:2-3

Describe your picture of the home being prepared for you. _____

_____

_____

_____

"Jesus answered and said to him, "If anyone loves Me, he will keep My word; and My Father will love him, and We will come to him and make Our _____ with him."
John 14:23

A Crown for His Princess!

"And everyone who competes for the prize is temperate in all things. Now they do it to obtain a perishable crown, but we for an _____ _____."
1 Corinthians 9:25

Life often feels like a competition. The world does not make it easy to live His way. What promise can you make yourself as you strive for your crown? _____

_____

_____

"...and when the Chief Shepherd appears, you will receive the crown of glory that does not _____ _____."
1 Peter 5:4

Material items in this life all perish with time. How do you feel knowing your heavenly reward can never fail? _____

_____

_____

*"I have fought the _____ fight, I have _____ the race,
I have _____ the faith. Finally, there is laid up for me the
crown of righteousness, which the Lord, the righteous Judge,
will give to me on that Day, and not to me only but also to all
who have loved His appearing."*
2 Timothy 4:7-8

Paul referred to his life as a fight, a race, showing the physical
endurance needed to keep going. It is a marathon, not a sprint. If
you start to get tired of fighting, how can you push yourself to
keep going? _____

_____

_____

*"For what is our hope, or joy, or crown of rejoicing? Is it not
even _____ in the presence of our Lord Jesus Christ at His
coming? For you are our glory and joy."*
1 Thessalonians 2:19-20

You are precious to God. You are His daughter. When you look
at yourself in the mirror, what do you see? _____

_____

_____

A princess is the crown jewel of the King!

*"No eye has seen, no ear has heard, and no mind has
_____ what God has prepared for those who love him."*
1 Corinthians 2:9 NLT

Daily Prayer and Journal Starters

Day 1 – Genesis 15:6-8

Sometimes we may find ourselves wondering about the promises of God. "How can I know that I will inherit it?" What can you draw from the life of Abraham? Is your faith encouraged that He will keep His promises to you? Read all of Genesis 15. What are your thoughts? What was God's response to Abraham's question in verse 8? If you ask questions of God, how do you think He would respond to you?

Day 2 – Exodus 34:8-9, 10-18

After the sin of the children of Israel with the golden calf (Genesis 32), Moses is preparing to receive the law a second time. He worships God and prays for God's forgiveness even though they are a stiff-necked or stubborn people. He prays that God still takes them as His inheritance (verses 8-9). In the rest of this section of Scripture, God spends time renewing His covenant. What do you think of God's offer and about the requirements placed on the people? What does God require of you as His child, His inheritance?

Day 3 – Numbers 27:1-11

God makes a special provision for the daughters of Zelophehad in regard to the inheritance of the Promised Land. He ensured that the women were not left out of what God had promised to His children. This is merely one example from Scripture where God shows His care and concern for women. Do you feel God's promises are as much for you as they are for others? Reflect on passages that make you feel secure in your inheritance and in the promises God has made you.

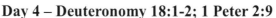

Day 4 – Deuteronomy 18:1-2; 1 Peter 2:9

The priests of God, everyone from the tribe of Levi, did not receive a portion of the land as an inheritance. What was given to them? If we are in Christ, what does Peter say we are? If we are part of the royal priesthood, what will be our inheritance? How do you feel knowing you are promised to inherit the Lord (all His promises, blessings, etc.)? Consider also David's thoughts in Psalm 16:5.

Day 5 – James 1:12; John 14:15

James tells us that those who love God will receive a crown of life if they continue to endure, to hold fast, to God during temptations. According to John, what will be our response if we love Him? God's promises often have conditions, just as you read earlier in Deuteronomy 34. If we love God, those conditions are not only something we endure, but they become something we are pleased to follow. How does love make this easier? If a promise has conditions, does it lessen the cost of the promised crown?

Day 6 – Hebrews 6:11-12

There are some strong action words that must be considered in these verses. If we are to "inherit the promises," we must not lose hope. What do words like diligence, faith, and patience suggest? When you feel like you are becoming a "sluggard" in your Christian walk, who can you imitate to keep you pressing forward?

Day 7 – 1 Peter 1:3-5

Consider how your inheritance is described in verse 4. Knowing that everything in this world fades, breaks, and is lost with time, does this description give you strength and encouragement? When you read that this inheritance is reserved in heaven for you, are you comforted knowing God is holding something special with your name on it?

Deeper Study

Carefully read and consider Psalm 139. As a daughter of the King, how well does God know you? If He knows you this well, does He know what is best for you? Spend some time meditating on what this passage says about God's relationship with you. Are you encouraged or concerned that God knows you so well? Take time to read this passage a few times. Make it personal, and see how much your Father loves you and knows you. Pray this passage. Thank God for loving you, His daughter, and for taking the time to think of you so often and know you so intimately.

J........ Joy for the Journey

> *"Whom having not seen you love. Though now you do not see Him, yet believing, you rejoice with joy inexpressible and full of glory." 1 Peter 1:8*

Most of us desire joy in our lives. We want that feeling of contentment and true peace, yet for many, it seems joy and peace are hard to find. Everyday problems wear us down. Heartaches, inconveniences, disappointments, overbooked schedules, can wear on us and rob us of our joy. We need a reminder of what true joy looks like and where we can find it. And not only that but how can we, amid all the constant negativity in the world around us, hold on to it!

We can get so bogged down with the "daily-ness" of our lives that we can lose sight of the joy that should be flowing through it because of our Father's love for us. Sometimes we all need reminders of the joy that is to be found in Christ. We need to learn to draw that joy from people around us and then learn to share it back again.

We are going to really look at what makes true joy. Through God's word, we will see what it is and what it isn't. Looking to Christ, let us discover how to have joy despite what the circumstances of our lives may dictate for us.

What Joy Is Not

Too many people in this world no longer know what true joy looks like, what it feels like in their lives. People seek quick bursts of happiness, momentary pleasures, thinking they are experiencing real joy, only to feel even worse when the euphoria fades and dwindles away. Joy is sought in the wrong places with the wrong expectations. So, what is true joy?

To know what true, godly joy is, we must first consider what it is not. Joy is not found in a laugh or a smile. Emotions can be falsely created by circumstances and quickly be removed. Joy is not so fleeting. It is not temporary, not a momentary feeling. Joy lasts and cannot be changed by a change in what is happening around us.

True and lasting joy is not found in worldly, material things. In fact, true joy is not found in this world at all. Jesus warned against laying up treasures in earthly things *"where moth and rust destroy and where thieves break in and steal"* (Matthew 6:19-21). He knew true joy could not be found in material possessions.

Lastly, and maybe most misunderstood, is the fact that real joy is not found in the absence of pain and suffering. Just because life is easy does not mean it is joyful. Likewise, because a life has hardships to bear does not mean it lacks joy. These two things are not always exclusive.

Joy is based on something more significant, something more profound than a life with no pain.

What is True Joy?

So, we have an idea of what real joy is not, but what is it? What makes real, true, and lasting joy in our lives? True joy comes from a place deep within, beyond emotions, beyond life's circumstances and changes. True joy is something that comes from God Himself and a relationship with Him. True joy is found in the presence of the Lord.

"You will show me the path of life; In Your presence is fullness of joy; At Your right hand are pleasures forevermore." Psalm 16:11

David recognized where true joy in life was found: with God. It wasn't found in his riches or his power. It wasn't found in

168

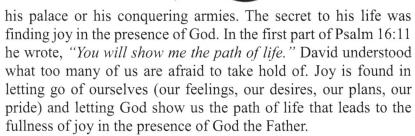

his palace or his conquering armies. The secret to his life was finding joy in the presence of God. In the first part of Psalm 16:11 he wrote, *"You will show me the path of life."* David understood what too many of us are afraid to take hold of. Joy is found in letting go of ourselves (our feelings, our desires, our plans, our pride) and letting God show us the path of life that leads to the fullness of joy in the presence of God the Father.

That joy in the presence of God is only found in a life believing in Christ and finding hope in the salvation He offers.

"In this you greatly rejoice, though now for a little while, if need be, you have been grieved by various trials, that the genuineness of your faith, being much more precious than gold that perishes, though it is tested by fire, may be found to praise, honor, and glory at the revelation of Jesus Christ, whom having not seen you love. Though now you do not see Him, yet believing, you rejoice with joy inexpressible and full of glory, receiving the end of your faith—the salvation of your souls." 1 Peter 1:6-9

Peter knew that although our lives would be *"grieved by various trials"* we would *"greatly rejoice"* with a *"joy inexpressible"* because of our love for Christ. That love would carry us through the trials and bring us joy. That joy would come from knowing that the end of our faith would find the salvation of our souls.

Christ is the reason we can have real joy that cannot be taken away by the world and its sorrows. Christ is the reason we can have joy in our hearts even if we don't have a smile on our face. The more we focus on the joy of Christ, the more it will grow in our lives.

"For I am persuaded that neither death nor life, nor angels nor principalities nor powers, nor things present nor things to come, nor height nor depth, nor any other created thing, shall be able to separate us from the love of God which is in Christ Jesus our Lord." Romans 8:38:39

Growing in Joy

Sometimes in our life, we may find we have lost our joy. The world has beat us down with blow after blow so much that the flame of joy for God that we once felt burn so hot, has become an ember on the verge of blowing out. How do we revive it? How do we strengthen ourselves spiritually by growing our joy?

Joy is a result of living after the Spirit of God. It takes work and practice, but that joy can bubble within us again if we are willing to live His way. Just as a fruit of a tree is the result of the tree living and growing, so are our spiritual fruits the results of our living and growing in God. Look at what it says in Galatians 5:22-23.

"But the fruit of the Spirit is love, joy, peace, longsuffering, kindness, goodness, faithfulness, gentleness, self-control. Against such there is no law." Galatians 5:22-23

When we live a life of obedience and faithfulness to God's Word, we will find these fruits growing in our lives. If we are lacking in a fruit, joy for example, then we need to do the things of God, think on the things of God that will help us grow in that area of our lives. John continues to expound on this idea in John 15:10-11.

"If you keep My commandments, you will abide in My love, just as I have kept My Father's commandments and abide in His love. These things I have spoken to you, that My joy may remain in you, and that your joy may be full." John 15:10-11

John reminds us of the close connection between abiding in the love of God by keeping His commandments. He says he spoke these things so our *"joy may be full."* Living by the commandments of God will lead us to true joy. The things that take away our joy in life are what God is trying to save us from.

The life God is guiding us toward will not only give us our joy in Him, but it will help us steer clear of many of life's pitfalls. Will following God mean we won't still have trials? No. Nor will it mean we may not suffer the consequences of other people's

170

lives and choices, but it will help you keep not only your joy but your connection with God.

Recognizing Joy

We can know and understand where true joy comes from but do we recognize it? Are we programming our hearts and minds to seek it and see it in our lives? There are many examples in scripture of people finding and recognizing joy in their lives. In fact, the word "joy" is used around 150 times throughout God's Word. That many times makes me believe that God wants us to recognize it and express it.

In the book of Exodus, we read of God's calling of Moses to go before Pharaoh in Egypt and call for the release of His people. After they witness the ten plagues and the destruction of Pharaoh and the Egyptian army from the other side of the Red Sea, the people sang and rejoiced before God for all He had accomplished to bring them salvation. (Exodus 15:1-22)

After all, they had witnessed and experienced, the Israelites took the time to rejoice and praise God. We too should never forget to look for those moments of joy, especially during and after hardships, to praise God with joy in our hearts. When we have come out the other side of our troubles, we need to recognize it and praise our Father for all He does for us.

Likewise, while in the midst of our troubles, we can learn from Paul and Silas not to lose our joy. In Acts 16:16-34, we read of them being thrown into a Philippian jail. These men were stripped of their clothes, beaten with rods, and had their feet fastened into stocks. While in the innermost part of the prison, Paul and Silas did not wallow in self-pity at their situation or treatment. No, in fact, the opposite is true for them.

These men sang. These men held a joy that rods and stocks could not steal from them. Verse 25 tells us that even at midnight after a long and rough day they were praying and singing hymns to God.

"But at midnight Paul and Silas were praying and singing hymns to God, and the prisoners were listening to them."
Acts 16:25

171

This is true, undeniable joy that the world cannot take away. This is joy the world does not understand and know. The world does recognize it as different, however. Notice how it says the prisoners were listening to them. They paid attention that there was something different about these men.

The other prisoners were not the only ones paying attention. By verse 34, not only has the jailer noticed the singing and praying of these men but the fact that when they had the chance to escape no one did. What could have been a life ending night (had prisoners escaped under his watch) turned into a life-changing night for him and his whole household.

"Now when he had brought them into his house, he set food before them; and he rejoiced, having believed in God with all his household." Acts 16:34

By the end of the night, not only were Paul and Silas rejoicing, but the jailer and his whole house were filled with real joy. Real joy cannot be contained, it must spread from one person to another. The joy found in God must come out where it affects those around you. It is life changing. It is powerful!

We must also consider the joy the joy of Peter's audience in 1 Peter 1 where he wrote that they greatly rejoiced though they had been grieved by various trials.

"In this you greatly rejoice, though now for a little while, if need be, you have been grieved by various trials, that the genuineness of your faith, being much more precious than gold that perishes, though it is tested by fire, may be found to praise, honor, and glory at the revelation of Jesus Christ, whom having not seen you love. Though now you do not see Him, yet believing, you rejoice with joy inexpressible and full of glory, receiving the end of your faith—the salvation of your souls." 1 Peter 1:6-9

These were brothers and sisters who had been persecuted and forced from their homes in the dispersion. These Christians now found themselves living in Pontus, Galatia, Cappadocia, Asia, and Bithynia (1 Peter 1:1). These were children of God who

had suffered for the cause of Christ but kept a joy that could not be taken from them even if everything else had been.

Or consider the Christians in Rome whom Paul addressed in Romans 5:1-5. They rejoiced in the hope of the glory of God and not only that but in tribulation, knowing the growth, it would bring to their lives.

"And not only that, but we also glory in tribulations, knowing that tribulation produces perseverance; and perseverance, character; and character, hope." Romans 5:3-4

Joy brings hope. Keeping joy in Christ keeps us going when we want to give us. There are so many examples in scripture we could turn to where people chose to recognize joy in their lives, even with circumstances were anything but joyful. There are people that I pray you take your time to consider and study. Examples such as Hannah who was barren and rejoiced over the blessing of her son (1 Samuel 2:1-11). Hannah, who as part of her rejoicing, gave her son to the service of God.

There was rejoicing at the dedication of the wall of Jerusalem (Nehemiah 12:43). There was rejoicing by Elizabeth and her unborn son John over the arrival of Mary the soon to be mother of Jesus in Luke 1:39-56. Then after the birth of Jesus, the angels in heaven rejoiced (Luke 2:13-14).

We are even told how the disciples found joy in the ascension of Jesus back to the Father and carried it with them to Jerusalem (Luke 24:50-53). As heartbroken as they were that He was gone from them in the flesh, they rejoiced. There is joy in Christ all around us if we train our eyes to look for it, look for the blessings, instead of the circumstances of the world. God has never failed to provide something in which we can find joy, we just need to learn to recognize it.

Do You Have True Joy?

The people in scripture had joy in good times and in bad. They kept the joy of God in their hearts where the world could not snatch it away. As a Christian, there should always be some measure of joy in your life. In times of life when it is good and easy and even when the road is rough and difficult to bear.

As a child of God, it should bring you joy to know that this world with all its sin and pain is not all there is for you. You have a home waiting in heaven, prepared by the Son of God Himself (John 14:1-3) where the troubles of this world can no longer reach you. Being from heaven, Jesus knew full well the joy of that home with the Father. It helped Him endure the trials and suffering here on earth. That same joy should drive you forward in your life.

"Therefore we also, since we are surrounded by so great a cloud of witnesses, let us lay aside every weight, and the sin which so easily ensnares us, and let us run with endurance the race that is set before us, 2 looking unto Jesus, the author and finisher of our faith, who for the joy that was set before Him endured the cross, despising the shame, and has sat down at the right hand of the throne of God." Hebrews 12:1-2

Verse one here in Hebrews 12 is an encouragement for us to look to that great cloud of witnesses recorded in Hebrews 11. For us to put aside every weight that ensnares us and tries to steal our joy. Once we can learn to lay those things down and look to God, we will recognize true joy. Remember that these pains and troubles in your life are fleeting. Whether they last for days, weeks, or even years, they are still temporary and will not follow you into eternity. The joy God offers, however, is everlasting.

"For His anger is but for a moment, His favor is for life;
Weeping may endure for a night, But joy comes in the morning."
Psalm 30:5

Choose joy. Rejoice always (1 Thessalonians 5:16). Rejoice in the Lord always and again (Philippians 4:4). Seek to focus on joy and not sorrow, realizing that the positives that God offers outweigh the negatives the world hurls. Joy is a matter of choice. It is a change of perspective. Strive for it. Seek it. Desire it. Hold on to it and never give it up.

Power Verse

"Blessed are the people who know the joyful sound! They walk, O Lord, in the light of Your countenance." Psalm 89:15

J....... Joy for the Journey

Worksheet

"Whom having not seen you love. Though now you do not see Him, yet believing, you rejoice with joy inexpressible and full of glory." 1 Peter 1:8

Do you have joy in your life? Explain why or why not.

_____

_____

_____

What Joy Is Not

What does the world often confuse for joy?

_____

_____

_____

Joy is not _____. It is not _____, not a _____ feeling.

Jesus instructed us to lay up treasure in _____ (Matthew 6:19-21).

Where do we typically think joy can be found?

_____

What is True Joy?

True joy is something that comes from _____ Himself and a _____ with Him.

"You will show me the path of life; In Your _____ is fullness of joy; At Your right hand are pleasures forevermore."
Psalm 16:11

David did not find joy in his wealth and possessions but found it with God. How does this compare with the ideas found in the world?

_____

_____

_____

Joy is found in letting go of and letting God show us the path of life that leads to the fullness of joy in His presence. Letting go of self is a challenge. What challenges do you find in letting go and letting God lead?

_____

_____

_____

"Though now you do not see Him, yet believing, you rejoice with joy _____ and full of _____, receiving the end of your faith—the salvation of your souls." 1 Peter 1:8-9

Trials can try to rob us of our joy. When the circumstances of life try to keep us from our joy, what are some things that can be focused on to find it again?

_____

_____

_____

"For I am persuaded that neither death nor life, nor angels nor principalities nor powers, nor things present nor things to come, nor height nor depth, nor any other created thing, shall be able to _____ us from the love of God which is in Christ Jesus our Lord." Romans 8:38:39

Nothing in this world can separate us from God. Describe these verses in Romans in your own words and what it means to you.

_____

_____

_____

Growing in Joy
Joy is a result of living after the _____ of God.

"But the _____ of the Spirit is love, _____, peace, longsuffering, kindness, goodness, faithfulness, gentleness, self-control. Against such there is no law." Galatians 5:22-23

How are the fruits in your life? Is there a fruit you need to grow in? How can you increase it?

_____

_____

_____

"If you keep _____ commandments, you will abide in _____ love, just as I have kept _____ Father's commandments and abide in His love. These things I have spoken to you, that _____ joy may remain in you, and that your joy may be full." John 15:10-11

There is one word that repeats in John 15:10-11. What is the connection to it and the joy God wants to be full in our lives?

_____

_____

_____

Recognizing Joy

The word "joy" is used around _____ times throughout God's Word.

Read of the joy of the people in Exodus 15:1-22. What stands out to you about their rejoicing?

_____

_____

_____

In Acts 16:16-34, Paul and Silas changed the life of the jailer and his whole house because of their rejoicing through trials. How can finding joy change your life?

_____

_____

_____

"But at midnight Paul and Silas were praying and singing hymns to God, and the prisoners were _____ to them."
Acts 16:25

It seems that most of the time people would rather spread bad news than good. What kind of changes would happen in our lives if we shared this kind of real joy with others? Would people listen to us?

_____

_____

_____

"Now when he had brought them into his house, he set food before them; and he _____, having _____ in God with all his household." Acts 16:34

There is a connection between real joy and belief in God. How does one affect the other?

_____

_____

_____

"In this you greatly rejoice, though now for a little while, if need be, you have been grieved by _____ _____, that the genuineness of your faith, being much more precious than gold that perishes, though it is tested by fire, may be found to praise, honor, and glory at the revelation of Jesus Christ, whom having not seen you love." 1 Peter 1:6-8

A life with joy does not mean a life without trials. What joy can come from trials?

_____

_____

_____

In Romans 5:1-5 tribulations produced several positive characteristics. Describe this process.

_____

_____

_____

"And not only that, but we also glory in tribulations, knowing that tribulation produces _____; and perseverance, _____; and character, _____." Romans 5:3-4

Read the scriptures for the following examples. Reflect over their joy in your own words.

Hannah - 1 Samuel 2:1-11

_____

_____

Children of Israel - Nehemiah 12:43

_____

_____

Elizabeth - Luke 1:39-56

_____

_____

The Angels - Luke 2:13-14

_____

_____

The Disciples - Luke 24:50-53

_____

_____

Do You Have True Joy?

What about God brings you joy?

_____

_____

"Therefore we also, since we are surrounded by so great a cloud of _____, let us lay aside every weight, and the sin which so easily ensnares us, and let us run with endurance the race that is set before us, looking unto Jesus, the _____ and _____ of our faith, who for the joy that was set before Him endured the cross, despising the shame, and has sat down at the right hand of the throne of God." Hebrews 12:1-2

Who are some examples of joy in your life?

_____

_____

_____

Jesus is the author and finisher of our faith? What does His life teach us about joy?

_____

_____

"For His anger is but for a_____, His favor is for _____; Weeping may endure for a night, But joy comes in the morning." Psalm 30:5

Trials are temporary, God's joy is _____! Choose _____!

Daily Prayer and Journal Starters

Day 1 – Psalm 5:10-12
David didn't take matters into his own hands but turned them over to God. He prayed for God to deal with those who sinned against him. He also prayed for those who were hurt to rejoice in defense of God. No matter our circumstance we should look to God for our true joy. Today write a prayer like David's in verse 12 and ask God to shield you from the circumstances in your life which burden your heart and for Him to help you see His joy in the midst of them.

Day 2 – Psalm 42:1-5, Psalm 122:1 & Hebrews 10:24-25
David felt distressed when he couldn't be near to worship God. He rejoiced to go to the house of God. The Hebrew writer encourages us not to forsake the assembly. God knows there is a joy to be found in His presence and in the presence of His people. What are your most joyful memories in worship?

Day 3 – Isaiah 61:10-11
God clothes us with the salvation of His Son. There is no greater joy than being in fellowship with God. If you have put on Christ in baptism and know the joy and peace it brings, write about your experience and what it has meant for you. If you have not, consider the life and joy He offers. Write out what Christ has done to bring true joy and what consider what is holding you back from accepting.

Day 4 – Habakkuk 3:17-19
Habakkuk, like many others in scripture, faced trying and difficult times. Even in the hard times, he was able to find joy in

God. Read this passage carefully and copy it down. Consider for yourself how Habakkuk was able to find joy in God. How do those ways apply to your life? What other ways do you find joy in the Lord?

Day 5 – Luke 15:1-10
When someone comes to God in faithful obedience, there is great rejoicing in heaven. Consider these two parables and the picture they offer of God. How do you feel knowing God's great joy when one of His children comes home?

Day 6 – John 16:16-22
A mother can easily relate to this image given by Jesus to His disciples of the pain of labor (the pain of them seeing their Lord crucified) is quickly forgotten when that tiny baby is placed in your arms (the joy they felt for the resurrected Savior). Verse 22 reminds us that this true joy in Christ can be taken away by no one. If you have children, let that be a reminder today of joy after pain. Let it remind you of Christ's love and the joy He brings. Describe that joy in your own words.

Day 7 – John 16:33
The fact that Jesus has overcome the world should strengthen us and bring us joy continually knowing that there is victory waiting for us. Focus on Jesus as the champion. He doesn't deny that we will have trouble in this world but desires for us to keep cheer in our hearts as we remember Him. How would you describe Jesus as the champion that brings joy to your heart?

Deeper Study

Read Psalm 106 carefully. Read it a few times. What attitudes stick out to you? What moments in history does David bring out? As David recounts some of Israel's sins, how does it make you feel about yourself or our nation? How does he describe the works of God? What feelings are stirred especially from verses 44-48 in comparison to all the negatives mentioned in the rest of the chapter? If God is willing to forgive the children of Israel for the sins listed here, what do you think He is willing to do for you?

K....... Know Your Foe

"Lest Satan should take advantage of us; for we are not ignorant of his devices." 2 Corinthians 2:11

Many people assume they know the enemy. We have heard the name. We have seen cartoon images depicting him. We think we have him all figured out, but the truth is that some do not really understand the real enemy. We are not prepared for the tactics he has mastered and the weapons he hurls. Why? Because he has tricked us into focusing our attention elsewhere.

This lesson will not focus on his origins and how he came to be, but rather it will be a guide to teach more about who he really is. Together we will look at how he works to cause so much damage in our lives. By knowing what he will try to use against the children of God, we can be more prepared to overcome him. When we know more about the enemy we are fighting, then we grow stronger spiritually to fight him more successfully.

Mistaken Identity

One important thing to keep in mind is who we should not be fighting: each other. We often mistake the identity of the enemy for those around us. When Paul is preparing the Christians at Ephesus to fight the right way with the right armor and weapons, he also writes to make sure they fight against the right enemy.

"Put on the whole armor of God, that you may be able to stand against the wiles of the devil. For we do not wrestle against flesh and blood, but against principalities, against powers, against the

rulers of the darkness of this age, against spiritual hosts of wickedness in the heavenly places." Ephesians 6:11-12

Paul wrote that we do wrestle against flesh and blood. The person who hurts you is not your real enemy. The man or woman who was rude to you bullied you, used you is not your enemy, even though it feels that way. As horrible as the actions of another can be to you, we must remember that they too are a creation of God who He seeks to save, they are not your enemy.

Free will gives everyone the freedom to choose their own actions, and sadly they may choose actions which are harmful to another. They may act without the knowledge of whose image they were created in and what purpose they were created for.

Think of the people at the foot of the cross screaming "Crucify Him." Think of the men who beat Christ and spit in His face. He was treated brutally and murdered and what was His response? It was not retaliation. It was not hatred for them as enemies. No, Christ responded with, *"Father, forgive them, for they do not know what they do."* (Luke 23:34)

Jesus understood that all those people were not His enemies, though their actions screamed otherwise, they were the very people He came to save. We too must learn to look at others the way Jesus does and not mistake them for the enemy but realize who we are really fighting against.

Paul went on to tell the Christians in Ephesus that the real fight was against, *"principalities, against powers, against the rulers of the darkness of this age, against spiritual hosts of wickedness in the heavenly places." (Ephesians 6:12)* He is reminding them, and us, that the enemy we must be focused on fighting is Satan, his followers, and the ideas and practices he perpetrates. He wants to make sure we don't mistake the identity of the enemy because knowledge of who we are fighting is power. When we are knowledgeable about the enemy and his devices, we can fight against him, and not be taken advantage of.

"Lest Satan should take advantage of us; for we are not ignorant of his devices." 2 Corinthians 2:11

186

Biblical Descriptions of Satan

There is quite a bit of information in scripture that we can learn from to make sure we have an accurate picture of who we are fighting. Knowing what to watch out for in our enemy will strengthen us against his attacks and learning to turn to God in those attacks will keep us strong!

In scripture, the devil, our enemy, is referred to in many ways. The name Satan as he is called in several texts is translated "Adversary" in both Hebrew and Greek. His very name suggests that he is our enemy, not to be trusted. But what else does God tell us about him?

Accuser of the Brethren

"Then I heard a loud voice saying in heaven, "Now salvation, and strength, and the kingdom of our God, and the power of His Christ have come, for the accuser of our brethren, who accused them before our God day and night, has been cast down."
Revelation 12:10

Our enemy is an accuser. He is always claiming that someone has committed an offense or that we have done something wrong. Being an accuser puts up walls of separation between God and us, it builds up the separation between ourselves and others. Having someone who constantly accuses us tears us down and makes us feel like we are worthless. Our accuser throws our mistakes back in our face when we are trying to move forward in our walk with Christ.

Having an accuser makes it hard to leave the past in the past. It makes it hard to build lasting relationships when there is an enemy whispering in your ear that trying to bring up mistakes and create mistrust. Our enemy, the adversary, uses this tool to break apart the bonds between God and us as well as us and those we are close to.

Tempter

"Again, the devil took Him up on an exceedingly high mountain, and showed Him all the kingdoms of the world and their glory."
Matthew 4:8

The enemy is a master tempter. Matthew 4 reveals to us that he stops at nothing and no one when it comes to temptation. Even our Lord and Savior was tempted by him. Satan hit Jesus at his weakest physical point after He had been fasting for forty days and forty nights. He attacked Him at what would be His most vulnerable points. This is what our enemy does to us as well.

Our enemy knows us, and that is why we need to know him. He knows when we are at our weakest and that is when he chooses to attack. He knows our weaknesses and exploits them to try and make us choose sin over God. Our enemy tempts us in, and we need to be prepared, so we do not fall into the temptation trap.

Liar & Murderer

"You are of your father the devil, and the desires of your father you want to do. He was a murderer from the beginning, and does not stand in the truth, because there is no truth in him. When he speaks a lie, he speaks from his own resources, for he is a liar and the father of it." John 8:44

This description affects us at such deep levels. Our enemy is a murderer from the beginning of time. The cause of death and destruction upon the whole earth. His expertise is death. Not only that he is a liar and the father of all lies. Lies that began in the garden when he turned God's words around and deceived Eve (Genesis 3). There is no truth to be found in him, and we must be careful not to fall prey to his lies.

This verse tells us so much about the very character of our enemy. He speaks lies from his own resources, all he knows is untruth and death. Our enemy will stop at nothing to bring us down. We must know him so we can learn to resist him.

"Therefore, submit to God. Resist the devil and he will flee from you." James 4:7

These are only a few of the descriptions God gives us of our enemy. He is also referred to as the wicked one (Matthew 13:38), the god of this world (2 Corinthians 4:4), and the prince of the power of the air (Ephesians 2:2). He has this world in his grips and has since his first appearance in the garden. We must be on

the lookout for him because he is constantly on the look out for his next target.

"Be sober, be vigilant; because your adversary the devil walks about like a roaring lion, seeking whom he may devour."
1 Peter 5:8

Tools and Tricks of Satan

From the beginning, Satan has used what ever tricks necessary to pull someone away from God. He makes people believe that what he is offering is better than the real life that God offers. This, of course, is never true because all Satan offers are lies. There are some tricks and tools that Satan uses to deceive us and the whole world (Revelation 12:9).

Confusion – *"For God is not the author of confusion but of peace, as in all the churches of the saints."* *1 Corinthians 13:33* – Paul wrote that confusion is not from God. Therefore the only option left is that it must be from Satan. What an effective tool he uses. Satan throws so much at people that they can't distinguish what is real and keep their focus on God. Instead, they are lost and turned around, so they do not know what to trust.

James tells us that confusion is part of false wisdom that does not descend from God above but instead is demonic. (James 3:13-16) He confuses us with what looks right, what looks spiritual, making things of this world seem right and confusing us to the truth of God's word! We must fight against this confusion and look to God for what is real. To study the original and not be confused by the counterfeit.

Blinding – *"But even if our gospel is veiled, it is veiled to those who are perishing, whose minds the god of this age has blinded, who do not believe, lest the light of the gospel of the glory of Christ, who is the image of God, should shine on them."* *2 Corinthians 4:3-4* – The devil blinds those who don't believe in God from seeing the truth of the Gospel. He uses his tricks to turn their minds from seeing the truth to keep them right where he

189

wants them, lost. Many times, Jesus used the phrases, "He who has eyes to see," because the people of the world have been so blinded by the tools of Satan that they cannot see the truth that is before them.

Appearing Good – *"And no wonder! For Satan himself transforms himself into an angel of light."* 2 Corinthians 11:14 – Paul wrote a warning to the church in Corinth that the devil and his angels try to appear as workers of righteousness. He and his agents appear as angels of light, minister of righteousness, basically wolves in sheep's clothing to slowly lure people away from God thinking they are doing what seems right. Everything we read and are taught, we must compare it to the truth of God's Word, the real light, so as not to be tricked by what appears to be light.

Hinders Us – *"Therefore we wanted to come to you—even I, Paul, time and again—but Satan hindered us."* 1 Thess. 2:18 – Satan hinders us any way he can. He places obstacles in front of us. He makes us doubt, fear, or give up so that we do not do what God asks. He makes our paths rough and full of temptations to keep us from obeying. When we sin, he convinces us that no one can love us any long, urging us to give up trying forever.

Traps & Snares – *"and that they may come to their senses and escape the snare of the devil, having been taken captive by him to do his will."* 2 Timothy 2:26 – Like quicksand, Satan traps us, and we begin to feel like we can't escape. We feel captive to the negative things around us. He sets up snares to catch us at our weakest points and tempts us into moving away from God. We must be aware when we feel ourselves being pulled in a way that we know will not lead us closer to God, that we are in a trap and must seek a way of escape. (Which we are blessed to know God always supplies. 1 Corinthians 10:13)

Satan uses all these tricks and more. He finds any way possible to turn us against each other and against God. He knows God will never let us go and that he is powerless to tear us away

190

from God's grasp, so he must trick us into leaving on our own. He deceives us into thinking we are missing something in this world. He deceives into thinking we are the enemies! He deceives us into believing those around us are our enemy.

How Jesus Handled Satan

When we know the tricks Satan uses against us, how can we be prepared to fight against him? What can we do to be ready to fight and not be caught unawares? We can start by looking at how Jesus handled Satan. Jesus was not overtaken by Satan's deceptions, and we can take comfort in knowing He has fought the big battles for us.

We can grow stronger in our spiritual walk when we recognize what Christ came to do not only for our sins but against our enemy. He came to earth with a purpose. He came to defeat the one who brought sin and death and remove His reign from this earth forever.

"He who sins is of the devil, for the devil has sinned from the beginning. For this purpose the Son of God was manifested, that He might destroy the works of the devil." 1 John 3:8

Jesus came to destroy the works of the devil. From the beginning, the devil has been about tearing God's children away from the Father. He has worked tirelessly from creation to build up barriers between God and us that seem immovable. But Jesus came to change all of that. Jesus came to break down the walls and destroy all that Satan has worked for.

Jesus came to be our sacrifice for sins, and it was promised from the garden that he would destroy the enemy. Genesis 3:15 foretold of Jesus that, *"And I will put enmity between you and the woman, and between your seed and her Seed; He shall bruise your head, and you shall bruise His heel."* The picture here is of a crushing blow to the head that would end the enemy. Something that could not be recovered from, while the enemy's bruise to the heel (the death on the cross) was for just a moment.

This was Christ's purpose from the beginning. To destroy Satan who had tried so hard to destroy the beautiful creation of

God. How wonderful to know that our Savior has already defeated our true enemy!

"Inasmuch then as the children have partaken of flesh and blood, He Himself likewise shared in the same, that through death He might destroy him who had the power of death, that is, the devil," Heb. 2:14

Christ's death rendered Satan powerless. When Jesus died on that cross, no doubt Satan rejoiced thinking he had finally won over God. But he could not have been further from the truth. The reality is, in that death, Christ took away the only real power Satan had, the power over death. He claimed it back and removed the fear of death from all those who believe and obey in the Son of God.

Jesus came to earth and took on flesh and blood, forever changing Himself to become like His creation. He suffered greatly at the hands of His creation, all to defeat our greatest enemy!

Matthew 4:1-11 is a very specific example of how Jesus handled Satan. Take the time to read this chapter and consider the response of Jesus after each temptation. Three times Satan attacked Him at His weakest point, offering to give Him something that would remove His pain in this world. Three times Jesus replied with "It is written." Turning to God's Word was how Jesus resister the tactics of Satan and it is the most powerful weapon we have against him as well.

How We Battle Satan

The most important thing to remember is that the war is over, it has already been decided who the victors are! God has won, and if we are His then we are on the winning team! Satan has been defeated. Even though the end has already been decided, we must still fight through the battles Satan places in our lives. But how? What can we do to battle against Satan and stay strong in our spiritual lives?

1. Stay Strong in God's Word – We just looked at in Matthew 4 where Jesus answered every temptation of Jesus by quoting the

Word of God. Matthew 4:5-6 shows us that Satan also knows God's word.

"Then the devil took Him up into the holy city, set Him on the pinnacle of the temple, and said to Him, "If You are the Son of God, throw Yourself down. For it is written: 'He shall give His angels charge over you,' and, 'In their hands they shall bear you up, Lest you dash your foot against a stone.'"

Satan tries to confuse us by turning it and twisting it to his own desires. The enemy knows our weapon well. We must know it for ourselves, we must be able to recognize what is real in his word and what may not be! He used this same trick with Eve in the garden, turning God's Word so that he could deceive her into thinking God was holding something back from her and urging her to sin.

Satan never has been an atheist. He has always believed in God and known God's Word, and he has tried to twist and pervert it to turn it into a weapon against us. We must know the Word of God better than our enemy. We must be students of it and keep it in our hearts and minds so we can answer Satan back truthfully with, "It is written."

2. Put on the Armor of God – Ephesians 6:11-18 gives us the weapons and defense for our battle against the ultimate enemy. When we take this passage seriously and look at the tools God gives us for battle, we can be prepared to fight and stand firm.

"Therefore take up the whole armor of God, that you may be able to withstand in the evil day, and having done all, to stand."
Ephesians 6:13

God, through Paul to the Ephesians, has told us to gird ourselves with truth. We cannot accept anything but the true doctrine of Christ. No other weapon will stand against the enemy. It must be wrapped around us protecting us and keeping everything in its rightful place. We are to protect our chest, our heart, with righteousness. Keeping our hearts pure and holy for

God's work.

To be complete, our armor must include feet ready to stand firm in the gospel of Christ and a shield of faith to protect us from the enemy's darts. God has given us the helmet of salvation to protect our minds from Satan's lies and the sword which is sharper than any blade. (Hebrews 4:12) These are the tools which God gives us to battle with so that we can be prepared to fight for our very would against the enemy.

3. Submit to God, Resist the Devil – To battle the enemy we have to surrender or submit to our King, our leader, who only wants the best for us. God is trying to protect you and bring you home with Him for eternity. To turn and resist the devil takes submitting our will to the Father's and trusting that He knows us, knows our past and our future, and He knows the ways that will bring us home.

"Therefore submit to God. Resist the devil and he will flee from you." James 4:7

4. Do Not Give Place to the Devil – In Ephesians 4:25-29, Paul gives practical advice to the children of God on how to resist the devil and not give him a place in our lives. If you give him an inch, he will take a mile as the old saying goes. In Paul's words of encouragement, he tells us to be angry but do not dwell on it. To give us stealing and corrupted speech. He is saying to put away anything that could give the devil a jumping point to get ahold of our hearts and our lives.

Do not give the devil a place to reside. Honor God with your actions and with your thoughts. Do not give him a home within in you and by doing so, you defeat him before he can start the fight. When we can resist the devil by not living in such ways as to give him a way in, then we live in a place of strength in battle, not of weakness.

Paul ends that passage by saying, *"be kind to one another, tenderhearted, forgiving one another, even as God in Christ forgave you." (Ephesians 4:32)* When God gives us tools to use for battle, he does so in a way that encourages those around us as well as reminds us why we are fighting to begin with. Because

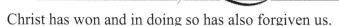

Christ has won and in doing so has also forgiven us.

The enemy has lots of tools and weapons at his disposal to use against us, but we have the strength of an all-powerful Lord God who has already won the battle for eternity. Let us draw from that power to know who our enemy is and how we can stand against him.

Power Verse

"Beloved, do not believe every spirit, but test the spirits, whether they are of God; because many false prophets have gone out into the world." 1 John 4:1

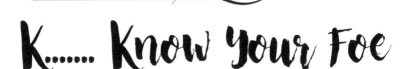

K....... Know Your Foe

Worksheet

"Lest Satan should take advantage of us; for we are not ignorant of his devices." 2 Corinthians 2:11

How would you describe an enemy?

_____

_____

_____

Mistaken Identity

"Put on the whole armor of God, that you may be able to stand against the wiles of the _____. For we do not wrestle against _____ and _____, but against principalities, against powers, against the rulers of the darkness of this age, against spiritual hosts of wickedness in the heavenly places."
Ephesians 6:11-12

In the verses above, who did Paul say we were not fighting against?

_____

_____

People around us often feel like our enemy because of their actions toward us. The people at the foot of the cross must have seemed like enemies to Christ. How were their actions different on the day of Pentecost in Acts 2?

_____

_____

_____

Christ forgave them because He knew who the real enemy was.

"Father, _____ them, for they do not know what they do."
Luke 23:34

Using Christ as our example, how are we to act to people who act as our enemy?

_____

_____

_____

If we do not know our foe, we risk falling victim to his deception. Describe the real enemy we face.

_____

_____

_____

"Lest Satan should take _____ of us; for we are not ignorant of his devices." 2 Corinthians 2:11

Biblical Descriptions of Satan
Define Adversary.

_____

_____

_____

Accuser of the Brethren
"Then I heard a loud voice saying in heaven, "Now salvation, and strength, and the kingdom of our God, and the power of His Christ have come, for the _____ of our brethren, who accused them before our God day and night, has been cast down." Revelation 12:10

Satan accuses us of many things. Why are accusations so bad?

_____

_____

_____

Tempter
"Again, the devil took Him up on an exceedingly high mountain, and showed Him all the kingdoms of the world and their glory."
Matthew 4:8

The enemy waits until we are weak and knows what temptations are strongest for each person. What tempts one may not tempt another. What is your worst temptation? How can you learn to resist it?

_____

_____

_____

Name the three ways Jesus was tempted in Matthew 4.

_____

_____

_____

_____

_____

Liar & Murderer
"You are of your father the devil, and the desires of your father you want to do. He was a _____ from the _____, and does not stand in the truth, because there is no truth in him. When he speaks a lie, he speaks from his own resources, for he is a _____ and the _____ of it." John 8:44

Satan lies to us just as he lies to many in scripture. Read Genesis 3 and explain his lie to Eve.

_____

_____

_____

"Therefore, submit to God. _____ the devil and he will flee from you." James 4:7

Our enemy is constantly on the lookout for those whose physical and spiritual lives are weak. What ways can you think of to help us be ready for his attacks?

_____

_____

_____

"Be sober, be vigilant; because your adversary the devil walks about like a roaring lion, _____ whom he may _____."
1 Peter 5:8

Tools and Tricks of Satan

Confusion – *"For God is not the author of confusion but of peace, as in all the churches of the saints."* 1 Corinthians 13:33

Describe confusion and how it could affect us spiritually.

_____

_____

_____

God does not give us confusion, what does he give us? What are your thoughts on his peace and his gifts in 2 Timothy 1:7?

_____

_____

_____

Blinding – *"But even if our gospel is veiled, it is veiled to those who are perishing, whose minds the god of this age has blinded, who do not believe, lest the light of the gospel of the glory of Christ, who is the image of God, should shine on them."* 2 Corinthians 4:3-4

How would you describe someone who was blinded by Satan?

_____

_____

_____

Appearing Good – *"And no wonder! For Satan himself* _____ *himself into an angel of light."* 2 Corinthians 11:14

What is an example of something appearing as right but being wrong or sinful?

_____

_____

_____

Hinders Us – *"Therefore we wanted to come to you—even I, Paul, time and again—but Satan* _____ *us."* 1 Thess. 2:18

What are some examples of how Satan can hinder us?

_____

_____

_____

Traps & Snares – *"and that they may come to their senses and escape the* _____ *of the devil, having been taken captive by him to do his will."* 2 Timothy 2:26

Do you have any advice for someone who has fallen into a trap of Satan?

_____

_____

_____

How Jesus Handled Satan
What was one of the purposes of Jesus coming in the flesh?

_____

_____

"He who sins is of the devil, for the devil has sinned from the beginning. For this _____ *the Son of God was manifested, that He might* _____ *the works of the devil."*
1 John 3:8

What prophecy was given in Genesis 3:15?

_____

_____

_____

"Inasmuch then as the children have partaken of flesh and blood, He Himself likewise shared in the same, that through death He might _____ him who had the _____ of _____, that is, the devil," Heb. 2:14

Christ's death rendered Satan _____.

What was Christ's answer to the temptations of the devil in Matthew 4?

_____

How We Battle Satan
What comes to mind when you think of each of these ways to battle Satan and his ways?

1. Stay Strong in God's Word –

_____

_____

_____

2. Put on the Armor of God –

_____

_____

_____

3. Submit to God, Resist the Devil –

_____

_____

_____

"Therefore _____ to God. Resist the devil and he will flee from you." James 4:7

201

4. Do Not Give Place to the Devil –

_____

_____

_____

What are some of the practical ideas Paul gives in Ephesians 4:25-29 for dealing with our brothers and sisters that can help us avoid giving place to the devil?

_____

_____

_____

Daily Prayer and Journal Starters

Day 1 – Ephesians 6:12
Our for wants to confuse us as to who is the real enemy we face. Often, we are confused, thinking those who wrong us are our enemy, but they too are just lost souls in need of a savior. The real enemy is Satan. Consider this verse and the differences in who we are really fighting. Do you always recognize the real enemy? Is it easy to get caught up in battles against those who are not our real enemies?

Day 2 – John 10:7-18
Think about what differences Jesus is pointing out here between Him, the good shepherd, and the thief. Do you know the good shepherd enough to recognize His voice? His truth? What can you do to better recognize Him and therefore be aware of anything that is not of Him?

Day 3 – James 4:7-10
James gives us strong words to help us when we are faced with the enemy. There are two directions for us – a resistance or running away from Satan and a running toward God, drawing ourselves ever nearer to Him. What are some ways you can accomplish this?

Day 4 – John 16:11, Matthew 25:31-46, & 1 John 3:8
Many are under the false impression that Satan is the ruler of Hell. That he will be over those souls, who chose that path in life, dishing out tortures over the condemned. Paying attention to Matthew 25:41, who has hell been prepared for? In contrast, how does this make you feel about God when you consider the words of Peter in 2 Peter 3:9?

Day 5 – Genesis 4:1-7

Don't believe the lie that you have no power over Satan and his temptations. You are more powerful than you know. Consider the words God spoke to Cain. Cain chose to give up his power and give over his control to temptation and anger. What steps can you take to empower yourself to "rule over sin?"

Day 6 – 1 John 2:15-17

The things Satan promises us and tempts us with are passing lies. They are passing away and will one day slip through our fingers and leave us with feelings of emptiness and regret. We will find ourselves trapped, longing for the next promise he offers. God calls us away from these things because to love them means we do not have the love of the Father. When we come to God out of the world, it means giving up on some things and taking on what Christ offers. Think today of all the true promises of Christ that are everlasting. Begin a blessing and promises list to encourage you to stay strong in the face of temptation.

Day 7 – Genesis 3:1-6

Satan is cunning. He strikes us in our weakest moments, in the weakest areas of who we are. He knows us well. He knows exactly which buttons to press to make us feel inadequate, unprepared, incapable, vulnerable. We need to be honest and truly know ourselves as well so we can strengthen these weak areas. As hard as it is, today be honest with yourself. Where are you the weakest? What are your more vulnerable spots that Satan will target? Once you identify them, what steps can you take to grow in these areas, so you can resist him even more?

Deeper Study

Revelation is a powerful book of pictures and Revelation 12:7-12 is no exception. This passage offers great hope as well as a powerful realization that God and Satan are not equals. They are not two sides of the same coin. It is such a false idea that too many fall victim to believing. In this picture notice that when

Satan and his angels attack heaven, God does not even get off His throne. Michael and the angels fought Satan and threw him out of where he didn't belong. Knowing that God is indeed all-powerful, how does this make you feel? What other pictures in scripture teach the true power of God? The book of Job is another great area to study and consider the limitations God set that Satan had no power to overcome.

.... Notes ....

L...... Love One Another

*"A new commandment I give to you, that you love one another;
as I have loved you, that you also love one another."
John 13:34*

Love is probably the most powerful human emotion. It gives us a strength we never knew we were capable of and at the same time can bring us to our most vulnerable of places. Love is a mighty motivator. Love is what sent our Savior, the very Son of God to this earth to die for us.

*"For God so loved the world that He gave His only begotten
Son, that whoever believes in Him should not perish but have
everlasting life." John 3:16*

God's love gave us the ultimate gift of heaven and in return asked that we show that love to others. Our obedience to God requires that we love those around us.

*"Beloved, let us love one another, for love is of God; and
everyone who loves is born of God and knows God. 8 He who
does not love does not know God, for God is love. 9 In this the
love of God was manifested toward us, that God has sent His
only begotten Son into the world, that we might live through
Him. 10 In this is love, not that we loved God, but that He loved*

207

*us and sent His Son to be the propitiation for our sins. 11
Beloved, if God so loved us, we also ought to love one another."
1 John 4:7-11*

This passage by John both opens and closes with the command for us to love one another. When scripture repeats something, especially in such a short section, it means the Holy Spirit wants us to pay attention – what is being said is important. It is essential that we love one another.

John continues in this section to make a connection between love and knowing God because God is love (verse 8). This is where some of us get lost, however, because God's love is so big that we don't know where to start. We understand that love should be behind everything that we do. That having the love of God in what shows the world that we are His children (John 13:35). But when it comes down to living in that love every day, what does it look like?

God's Love is Different from the World's Love

To understand God's love and be able to live it in our lives we must know that it is not what the world views as love, God's love is different. It causes us to be different, to live differently, act and think differently. How is God's love different? There are a few areas in particular to consider.

- God's Love Doesn't Expect Anything in Return
Read passages like Luke 6:30-36 and Luke 14:12-14 and you will see a love that is given without seeking anything in return. God's love is free to all. There is no hidden agenda or self-seeking, but rather a desire to lift others up and make sure their needs are met.

- God's Love Seeks Others' Needs First
Look at Philippians 2:1-5. We are to esteem others' needs and seek their best interests. By doing so, we are having the mind of Christ who gave up everything for our betterment. Christ came to earth, giving up His place in Heaven, to walk these

streets, be rejected and humiliated but the very people He came to save, all in love.

- God's Love Loves Without Judgment
When we read James 2:8-9 we see that God's love does not deem one person as more deserving than another. God's love realizes that every person we see was created in His image and deserving of our love. This is true whether the person realizes it or not, acts like it or not. When Jesus was on earth, He went to the people the world had deemed worthless and showed them God's lovingkindness. This is our call – to love as God loved and that means everyone without judgment and partiality.

- God's Love Loves His Enemies
Take a moment to read Romans 12:9-21 and Matthew 5:43-48. God's love doesn't stop with those who are different or downtrodden but reaches out to those who would be our enemies and seem unlovable. Aren't we glad God loves His enemies!

"For if when we were enemies we were reconciled to God through the death of His Son, much more, having been reconciled, we shall be saved by His life." Romans 5:10

If God's love did not stretch out toward His enemies, then none of us would be able to call ourselves His children. We all have sinned (Romans 3:23) and were dead in those sins (Ephesians 2:1-6), but His love saved us when we were enemies and powerless to save ourselves.

Yes, undeniably yes, God's love stands distinctly different from the world's idea of love. The world views of love are selfish and childish. If it makes me happy, then it must be love. If it agrees with me, it's love. If it doesn't cost me to give of myself, it's love. No, the world does not define love in the same way as God. So how is God's love defined?

Defining God's Love

Perhaps no chapter in all of God's Word defines God's love, the love that we are to have for one another, better than 1 Corinthians 13. These 13 short verses give us the expectations and view of what godly love is all about.

"Though I speak with the tongues of men and of angels, but have not love, I have become sounding brass or a clanging cymbal.
2 And though I have the gift of prophecy, and understand all mysteries and all knowledge, and though I have all faith, so that I could remove mountains, but have not love, I am nothing.
3 And though I bestow all my goods to feed the poor, and though I give my body to be burned, but have not love, it profits me nothing.
4 Love suffers long and is kind; love does not envy; love does not parade itself, is not puffed up;
5 does not behave rudely, does not seek its own, is not provoked, thinks no evil;
6 does not rejoice in iniquity, but rejoices in the truth;
7 bears all things, believes all things, hopes all things, endures all things.
8 Love never fails. But whether there are prophecies, they will fail; whether there are tongues, they will cease; whether there is knowledge, it will vanish away.
9 For we know in part and we prophesy in part.
10 But when that which is perfect has come, then that which is in part will be done away.
11 When I was a child, I spoke as a child, I understood as a child, I thought as a child; but when I became a man, I put away childish things.
12 For now we see in a mirror, dimly, but then face to face. Now I know in part, but then I shall know just as I also am known.
13 And now abide faith, hope, love, these three; but the greatest of these is love." 1 Corinthians 13

After just discussing spiritual gifts in chapter 12, Paul takes a step back to explain to us the greatest gift of all. The gift we are commanded to bestow on others. Without this kind of love our actions and our gifts are nothing and profit us nothing (verses 1-3). God's love must be the driving force behind our obedience of all His commands, and it must be what pushes us to seek the best for those around us. How can we know if it is God's love?

210

- Verse 4 – God's love suffers long. It bears with others and does it give up on them. It treats them with kindness and does not envy their successes. When we succeed, the love of God does not parade our success in the face of others, puffing ourselves up, seeking to make others jealous with what we have done.
- Verse 5 – God's love has respect in how it treats everyone, and it does not behave rudely, even when traffic is slow, or it is bumped in the grocery line. It does not seek out only for itself, being provoked into anger or hatred, thinking no evil of others, only the best.
- Verse 6 – God's Love seeks only truth, and as such it does not rejoice when others mess up and miss the mark. God's love offers to help the one who stumbles to stand again without running to tell others about their fall.
- Verse 7 – The love of God that we are to have for others bears all things. It holds up under anything that comes and does not give up. God's love puts up with things for love's sake. It believes the best in everyone, hoping without fail under any circumstance, enduring to the end.
- Verse 8 – When everything else in this world fails and falls apart – God's love will remain. God's love lasts forever. It never stops because it gets hurt or upset. God's love outlasts everything in this whole world.

These are the differences in God's defining love that He calls His children to show to one another. Can you imagine a world that was full of this kind of love? A world where there were no crimes because love wouldn't harm another person. A world where there were no harsh words or disappointments because love for someone else meant putting them first.

This is the love God calls you to strive for. This is the love God not only spoke about and defined but put on flesh to show us first hand what it looked like in action.

God's Love in Action

As if defining the love of God was not enough, God showed us the perfect example of loving others God's way. John 13:1-7 is

211

a beautiful picture of our Lord showing us how to live a 1 Corinthians 13 kind of love toward one another.

Jesus knew that His time on earth was nearing the end and verse one says He loved His own until the end. Breaking the traditions and attitudes of the respected leaders, Jesus rose from the feast and girded Himself with a servant's towel (verse 4). Jesus, knowing who He was, where He was from and where He was going (verse 3) lowered Himself to the place of a servant. The King of Kings, Lord of all creation, did not think Himself above those He came to serve, but lowered Himself and began to wash the feet of His disciples.

This tradition was typically done by a servant or by the socially lowest person in the house once everyone entered. Wearing sandals and walking the dusty roads left one's feet dirty and uncomfortable. Yet, here it was after supper (verse 2), and none of the disciples had taken it upon themselves to care to the needs of the group.

This is too often us. We will do a lot of things for others but to lower ourselves to such a menial task becomes difficult. We all want to be appreciated, be someone important that others respect and look up to, and it can be hard to lower ourselves, even for the good of others.

But God's love doesn't seek itself, it seeks for the needs of others to be met no matter what, without partiality. After this moment in the lives of Jesus and the disciples, Jesus is going to talk about His betrayer. Yet, while Jesus is washing the feet of the disciples, he does not treat Judas any differently. No one else in the group knows who the betrayer is because the love of God is the same for all.

Jesus led them, and us, by a beautiful example. He asks, *"Do you know what I have done for you?"* (Verse 12) Jesus showed them how to love. Jesus showed us how to love. He said, *"I have given you an example, that you should do as I have done to you."* (verse 15)

The love of God for our brothers and sisters compels us to act, to serve. Loving one another is sometimes dirty and uncomfortable. Loving as Christ loved sometimes means saying

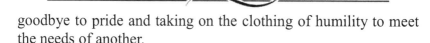

goodbye to pride and taking on the clothing of humility to meet the needs of another.

God is sending us into the world to show and share His love. God commands that we are to love everyone. God showed us how to do it and said, *"If you know these things, blessed are you if you do them."* (Verse 17) God's love is living and active in you for you to share with others!

Power Verse

"By this all will know that you are My disciples, if you have love for one another." John 13:35

L....... Love One Another

Worksheet

"By this all will know that you are My disciples,
if you have love for one another."
John 13:35

What motivated God to send His Son? _____

"For God so _____ the world that He gave His only
begotten Son, that whoever believes in Him should not
perish but have everlasting life."
John 3:16

How many times is the word love used in the following verses?

"Beloved, let us _____ one another, for _____ is of God;
and everyone who _____ is born of God and knows God.
8 He who does not _____ does not know God, for God
is_____. 9 In this the _____ of God was manifested toward
us, that God has sent His only begotten Son into the world,
that we might live through Him. 10 In this is _____, not
that we _____ God, but that He _____ us and sent His
Son to be the propitiation for our sins. 11 Beloved, if God
so _____ us, we also ought to _____ one another."
1 John 4:7-11

If it is important enough to repeat that many times, how important must love to God? How important should it be to us?

_____

_____

"By this _____ will _____ that you are My disciples, if you have love for one another." John 13:35

How are we recognized by the world?

_____

_____

When it comes down to living in that love every day, what does it look like?

_____

_____

God's Love is Different from the World's Love
Read the following passages and record your thoughts about God's love.

- God's Love Doesn't Expect Anything in Return - Luke 6:30-36 and Luke 14:12-14

_____

_____

_____

- God's Love Seeks Others' Needs First - Philippians 2:1-5

_____

_____

_____

- God's Love Loves Without Judgment - James 2:8-9

_____

_____

_____

- God's Love Loves His Enemies - Romans 12:9-21 and Matthew 5:43-48.

_____

_____

_____

Defining God's Love
Read 1 Corinthians 13 again. Personalize it by writing it in your own words.

_____

_____

_____

_____

_____

_____

_____

_____

_____

_____

_____

Read it again, this time replace the word Love with your name. Are these things true in your life? Do you show this kind of love?

God's Love in Action
Read John 13:1-7. What Jesus did to show love in action was not a big extravagant event. It was simply meeting the needs of someone else.

What are some ways you can meet the needs of others and show them the love of God? Be specific.

_____

_____

_____

Look at Peter's reaction to the Lord wanting to wash his feet. When someone shows lovingkindness to you, what is your typical reaction?

_____

_____

_____

Jesus asked, *"Do you know what I have done for you?"* (John 13:12) Describe what the love of Christ has done in your life?

_____

_____

_____

Jesus also said, *"I have given you an example, that you should do as I have done to you."* (John 13:15) Physical examples are powerful teachers and motivators. Who has been a powerful example of God's love in your life?

_____

_____

_____

"If you know these things, blessed are you if you do them." (John 13:17) How are we blessed by showing God's love to others?

_____

_____

_____

Daily Prayer and Journal Starters

Day 1 – 1 John 3:10-15

Loving one another is a serious charge that God has placed on His children. This scripture connects not loving our brothers and sisters with abiding in death. Love is a life and death commandment. It is love that separates the children of God from the children of the devil. The example given here is of Cain and Able. Read Genesis 4 as you prayerfully consider your own life. Is there a lack of love? Are there grudges or strife keeping you from loving as God loves? What can you do to resolve this issue?

Day 2 – Leviticus 19:17-18 & Romans 12:19

Love does not take vengeance or hold a grudge but trusts God to take care of both us and those who have wronged us. How do you love your neighbor through wrongdoings?

Day 3 – John 15:9-17

Jesus compares His love for the Father with the love He desires for us to have. Twice here He tells us to abide in His love. He wants us to make our home in the love He has for the Father and for us. There is safety and joy to be found in abiding in that love. He tells us that loving means keeping His commandments and that commandment is to love one another. How can abiding in the love of Christ help accomplish this?

Day 4 – 1 John 3:16-23

This passage calls on love in action, not just in words. John uses the example of Christ laying down His life for us and says we should do likewise for our brothers and sisters. Most of us will never be asked to physically give up our life for another. How

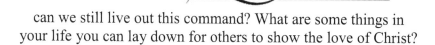

can we still live out this command? What are some things in your life you can lay down for others to show the love of Christ?

Day 5 – 1 John 4:17-19

How beautiful to know there is no fear to be found in God's perfect love. Verse 17 says love is perfected among us when we are like Christ in the world. This love of Christ gives us boldness in the day of judgment. If we love because He first loved us, giving the perfect example of what that looks like in the world, how do we show that love in our lives? Reflect on what that perfect love means to you.

Day 6 – Hebrews 13:1-3

We may never know the true impact our love for others will have in their lives. Verse 3 says we are to remember others as if we are the ones in their situation. How does putting ourselves in other's shoes affect our ability to show love for them?

Day 7 – 1 John 4:20-21

Love for God cannot flow from a heart filled with hate for someone else. How can we say we love our Creator if we hold hatred for His creation? Verse 21 says we <u>must</u> love our brothers and sisters. Sometimes this can be a challenge. If there is someone in your life, you find difficult to love spend today in prayer asking God to help you see positives in that person.

Deeper Study

Read and consider the following scriptures: Deuteronomy 6:5; Deuteronomy 10:12-13; Matthew 22:36-40; Mark 12:29-31; and Luke 10:26-28. These commandments are referred to as the Greatest Commands which Jesus says all the other laws and prophets hang upon. There are three commands to love given by Jesus: to Love God, Love Others, Love Self. Look for other passages that speak to these ideas of love. Make a list of your own reasons to love each of them. Especially consider why Jesus said to love others as yourself. If we do not have a healthy love for ourselves, does that hinder our ability to love others as God commands?

M....... Meditate on God's Word

"Let the words of my mouth and the meditation of my heart Be acceptable in Your sight, O Lord, my strength and my Redeemer." Psalm 19:14

Meditation can be a confusing word. It is used differently by other cultures, and the practice of meditating may not be something you ever considered to help strengthen your spiritual life. Biblical meditation on God's Word is quite different from the ideas of the world however and can be useful to keep us connected with God when we cannot be sitting at His feet in study.

Biblical meditation is not the emptying of your mind, but rather the filling of your mind, focusing your mind on the things of God. Meditating on God's Word requires effort to change your thoughts to remember God is always with you. It is acknowledging His presence daily and communicating with Him always.

Biblical Examples of Meditating

For many centuries, followers of God did not have access to the written word of God like we are blessed with today. Copying the scrolls word by word was done by hand and was very time-consuming. This made copies of God's Word expensive and precious and not every person had the ability to have them. Many may go their whole lives without seeing one themselves. To help

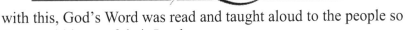

with this, God's Word was read and taught aloud to the people so they could learn of their Lord.

If God's people could not stay in active study with scripture, how did they stay focused on His Word? By memorizing it, by sharing it and talking about it with others, and by singing hymns to keep their minds on Him.

One of my favorite passages of scripture concerning this very idea comes from Deuteronomy 6. Moses is about to give the law of God to the people a second time as they prepare to enter the promised land. He tells them God has given these statutes to teach them, so they may observe these things when they possess the land (verse 1). He then tells them how they are to use God's Word in their lives.

"And these words which I command you today shall be in your heart. 7 You shall teach them diligently to your children, and shall talk of them when you sit in your house, when you walk by the way, when you lie down, and when you rise up. 8 You shall bind them as a sign on your hand, and they shall be as frontlets between your eyes. 9 You shall write them on the doorposts of your house and on your gates." Deuteronomy 6:6-9

After reminding them to love God with the whole of their being (verse 4-5), he sums up every part of their day. They are to have God's Word in their heart (memorization). They are to teach what they learned to their children (responsibility to share) talking about it when they were sitting in their home or walking outside. They were to talk about God when they went to bed at night and when they arose the next morning.

God covers every part of the day and no matter where they may be, and whatever they may be doing. They were at all times to be thinking about and talking about God and His Word.

This passage goes on to say they were to bind His Words on their hands and as frontlets between their eyes. The children of Israel would copy down passages of scripture and wear them on their bodies as constant reminders of what God had done for them and what He had commanded them.

Moses also instructed them to keep God's Word written on

the door posts of their homes and on their gates. These were visible reminders placed where they would be seen any time they were leaving or coming home. They were to keep God's Word in the forefront of their mind. This is biblical meditation. This is what is meant by meditating on God's Word.

Other's in scripture spent time meditating and focusing on God as well. Mary, the mother of Jesus, is said least twice, to have kept the words of God concerning her son in her heart, pondering on them and considering their meaning. After His birth when the shepherds came to see Jesus, we read, *"But Mary kept all these things and pondered them in her heart."* (Luke 2:19) Likewise, after they found 12-year-old Jesus at the temple and she heard the words of the teachers, "When He went down with them and came to Nazareth, and was subject to them, but His mother kept all these things in her heart." (Luke 2:51)

Here was Mary with a newborn and with a preteen. A busy mom who like most of us probably did not have much time to sit and study, yet she kept the words in her heart and mind and focused on the things of God.

Isaac also seemed to be in the habit of meditating. He sought out a quiet place to sit and focus. It was during one of these moments when he looked up to see the arrival of his future bride. *"And Isaac went out to meditate in the field in the evening; and he lifted his eyes and looked, and there, the camels were coming."* (Genesis 24:63)

Perhaps the greatest example of meditating on God's Word comes from David, the man after God's own heart (1 Samuel 13:14 and Acts 13:22). David who was willing to stand before the giant in 1 Samuel 17, straight out of his father's fields where he tended the sheep obviously had a strong relationship with God already. Looking at the Psalms, he wrote in his later life, and how many times he talks about meditating on God's Word, one can only think that this was a practice he held from his youth.

"Blessed is the man who walks not in the counsel of the ungodly, Nor stands in the path of sinners, nor sits in the seat of the scornful; 2 But his delight is in the law of the Lord, and in His law he meditates day and night. 3 He shall be like a tree planted

223

by the rivers of water, that brings forth its fruit in its season,
Whose leaf also shall not wither; and whatever he does shall
prosper." Psalm 1:1-3

God's Word was a central part of David's life, but there were times in his life, much like in ours, when he wasn't able to sit and study. Whether in the field with the sheep, in caves hiding for his life, or fighting in many wars, David had to keep his mind focused on God in every way that he could.

This should encourage us to know that no matter what is happening in our daily lives, we can meditate on God's Word and be connected with Him. David also wrote in Psalm 77 of his meditation and what he says can help us in our lives.

"And I said, "This is my anguish; but I will remember the years
of the right hand of the Most High." 11 I will remember the
works of the Lord; Surely I will remember Your wonders of old.
12 I will also meditate on all Your work, And talk of Your
deeds." Psalm 77:10-12

Three times in those verses he used the word remember. David would think of God's works, he would remember the wonders of old that God had worked for His people. David took these stories and events of the Most High with him and thought of them, meditated on them and talked with others about them.

This is something that every one of us can do every day. We can think about God and remember what He has done not only in our lives but in the lives of those recorded throughout scripture. We can remember them and share them with others.

Benefits of Meditating on God's Word

As we learn to meditate on God's Word, it is encouraging to know there are many benefits to staying connected to God regularly. God's Word is a powerful tool and the more we can be in it and spend dwelling on it, the more it will help and strengthen our lives.

"All Scripture is given by inspiration of God, and is profitable for doctrine, for reproof, for correction, for instruction in righteousness, 17 that the man of God may be complete, thoroughly equipped for every good work." 2 Timothy 3:16-17

God's Word is profitable for us in many ways. It corrects us as well as instructs us in righteousness. It makes us well equipped to live after Him. It makes us complete, whole, as we learn to lean on the Father. As we meditate on it, we will find other benefits as well.

- Keeps Us Connected to God – *"Pray without ceasing." 1 Thessalonians 5:17*
  As we begin learning to meditate, the easiest way to connect to God in prayer without ceasing. This doesn't always have to be an eyes closed on your knees with your head bowed moment for you to connect with Him. In fact, Jesus can read your thoughts (Psalm 139:1-6 and Matthew 9:4), so all we have to do is think on Him, connect with Him through focusing our thoughts and speak to God.

- Helps Us To Teach & Encourage Others – *"Let the word of Christ dwell in you richly in all wisdom, teaching and admonishing one another in psalms and hymns and spiritual songs, singing with grace in your hearts to the Lord." Colossians 3:16*
  By having the Word of God continually on our hearts and minds, we benefit by being ready and able to share it with others. This verse specifies that we are to let it dwell in us richly, abundantly, not sparingly. God's Word should flow from us with grace in our hearts to the Lord.

- Protects Our Hearts from Sin – *"Your word I have hidden in my heart, that I might not sin against You."* Psalm 119:11
  Keeping God's Word hidden in our heart helps strengthen us against temptations. The more we meditate on God's Word, not only will there be less time for sinful thoughts, but we will have the extra support of the scripture to say NO to things we

225

know are against God, keeping our hearts, minds, and lives pure.

- Keeps us in Peace – *"You will keep him in perfect peace, whose mind is stayed on You, because he trusts in You."* Isaiah 26:3
  When we meditate on God and His Word, we have the benefit of His peace to calm and comfort us. The peace of God is strong, and it can ease our fears and calm our anxieties. It can help us remember that He is in control when our lives seem to be anything but in control. Meditation on God's Word connects us to the peace which passes understanding (Philippians 4:7) which will guard our hearts and minds.

There are so many benefits we could continue with when it comes to meditating on God's Word regularly, but how do we do it? What does it look like in action in our lives daily?

How to Meditate on God's Word
There are many ways you can learn to meditate on God's Word daily to strengthen yourself spiritually. We can follow the examples of scripture and make them our own.

- Surround Yourself with God's Word – Deuteronomy 6:6-9
  As we looked in Deuteronomy 6, the children of Israel were to surround themselves with God's Word. There were constant reminders to switch their focus back to the Lord. They had scripture on their bodies and clothing and all around their homes.
  Use this to your advantage as well. Keeping memory verses in high traffic areas of your home – by the door, in your car, on the refrigerator, on your cell phone's home screen. Anything that you see regularly can help you think about God. Keep a sticky note on your bathroom mirror or on your computer monitor. Notice these verses, take time to read them and reflect. Let them remind you to pray and connect with God.

- Focus on the Positives – Philippians 4:8-9

Paul wrote to the Philippians to encourage them to think on anything praise worthy. Look for those things in your day. Let them help you see the blessings of God all around you. When bad things happen that drag you down, purposely focus your attention to see the good.

- Write the Word of God – Deuteronomy 17:18-20
Later in the book of Deuteronomy, long before there was the talk of kings in Israel, God commanded each king to write their own copy of the Word of God. He was to write it and read it every day so he would learn to fear the Lord and obey Him as he ruled God's people.
Writing God's word is an effective memorization tool. It physically connects you with the Word of God and secures stronger paths in your mind for it. Keep a journal and copy scripture. Write our memory verses on note cards to use for memorization. Practice writing God's Word to help you relax and reconnect with God.

- Memorize Scripture – Joshua 1:8-9
Joshua, when preparing to take over as leader of God's people after Moses, was directed by God that the book of the law was not to depart from his mouth. He was to know it and repeat it to the people. It needed to become part of him, so he could obey everything written in it and lead the people in the paths of God.
When we memorize God's Word, we take Him with us where ever we go. Nothing can take His Word away or hinder us from focusing on it. Start with a few verses, write them down, repeat them out loud, work at memorizing them and training yourself to think of them often.

- Praise God Continually – Psalm 71:5-8
Keep a song of praise on your heart and on your lips. Thank God for His blessings in your life and praise Him for being the Mighty Lord He is. David wrote that God was his trust from his youth and that he was filled with praise and glory of God all day.

227

Think of your favorite hymns. Sing to the Lord in the car or while washing the dishes (or whatever your hands find to do). Listen to songs of praise as you go about your day and let them encourage you in the Lord.

- Be Still – Psalm 46:10
  Perhaps one of the best ways to meditate on God's Word is one that in today's world we find so challenging to accomplish. Find time to be still and focus on the fact that God is God. Remind yourself of who He is and what that means for your life.

There is so much that could be said about meditating on God's Word. It is such a wonderful way to draw strength for your spiritual life. Be encouraged by the words of David as you learn to make meditation on God's Word a part of your daily routine.

"Oh, how I love Your law! It is my meditation all the day. 98 You, through Your commandments, make me wiser than my enemies; For they are ever with me. 99 I have more understanding than all my teachers, For Your testimonies are my meditation. 100 I understand more than the ancients, Because I keep Your precepts. 101 I have restrained my feet from every evil way, That I may keep Your word. 102 I have not departed from Your judgments, For You Yourself have taught me. 103 How sweet are Your words to my taste, Sweeter than honey to my mouth! 104 Through Your precepts I get understanding; Therefore I hate every false way."
Psalm 119:97-104

Power Verse

"I will meditate on the glorious splendor of Your majesty, And on Your wondrous works." Psalm 145:5

M...... Meditate on God's Word

Worksheet

"Let the words of my mouth and the meditation of my heart
Be acceptable in Your sight,
O Lord, my strength and my Redeemer." Psalm 19:14

How would you describe meditation?

_____

_____

_____

Biblical Examples of Meditating
What challenges did followers of God place for centuries?

_____

_____

_____

"And these words which I command you today shall be in
_____ _____. 7 You shall _____ them diligently to
your children, and shall _____ of them when you _____ in
your house, when you _____ by the way, when you _____
down, and when you _____ ____. 8 You shall _____ them as
a sign on your hand, and they shall be as frontlets between your
eyes. 9 You shall _____ them on the doorposts of your house
and on your gates." Deuteronomy 6:6-9

What stands out to you most about Deuteronomy 6:6-9?

_____

_____

_____

How often were the children of Israel to talk and think about God?

_____

_____

_____

In what ways do you feel a connection to these examples in scripture who meditated and focused on God's Word?

Mary, the mother of Jesus - Luke 2:19 & Luke 2:51

_____

_____

_____

Isaac - Genesis 24:63

_____

_____

_____

David –

_____

_____

_____

"Blessed is the man who walks not in the counsel of the ungodly, Nor stands in the path of sinners, nor sits in the seat of the scornful; 2 But his _____ is in the law of the Lord, and in His law he _____ on it _____ and _____. 3 He shall be like a tree planted by the rivers of water, that brings forth its fruit in its season, Whose leaf also shall not wither; and whatever he does shall prosper." Psalm 1:1-3

What encouragement can you gain from David?

_____

"And I said, "This is my anguish; but I will _____ the years of the right hand of the Most High." 11 I will _____ the works of the Lord; Surely I will _____ Your wonders of old. 12 I will also meditate on all Your work, And talk of Your deeds." Psalm 77:10-12

How important is it to remember the Word of God?

_____

_____

_____

Benefits of Meditating on God's Word
Name some of the ways scripture is profitable for our lives?

_____

_____

_____

"All Scripture is given by inspiration of God, and is profitable for _____, for _____, for _____, for _____ in righteousness, 17 that the man of God may be _____, thoroughly equipped for every good work." 2 Timothy 3:16-17

Reflect on the following benefits to meditation.
- Keeps Us Connected to God – *"Pray without ceasing." 1 Thessalonians 5:17*

_____

_____

- Helps Us To Teach & Encourage Others – *"Let the word of Christ dwell in you richly in all wisdom, teaching and admonishing one another in psalms and hymns and spiritual songs, singing with grace in your hearts to the Lord." Colossians 3:16*

231

_____

_____

_____

- Protects Our Hearts from Sin – *"Your word I have hidden in my heart, that I might not sin against You."* Psalm 119:11

_____

_____

_____

- Keeps us in Peace – *"You will keep him in perfect peace, whose mind is stayed on You, because he trusts in You."* Isaiah 26:3

_____

_____

_____

How to Meditate on God's Word

For each method listed, write some ideas that would work for you personally to help you meditate on God's Word daily.

- Surround Yourself with God's Word – Deuteronomy 6:6-9

_____

_____

- Focus on the Positives – Philippians 4:8-9

_____

_____

- Write the Word of God – Deuteronomy 17:18-20

_____

_____

- Memorize Scripture – Joshua 1:8-9

_____

_____

_____

- Praise God Continually – Psalm 71:5-8

_____

_____

_____

- Be Still – Psalm 46:10

_____

_____

_____

Daily Prayer and Journal Starters

Day 1 – 1 Timothy 4:15
When giving instruction to Timothy as a minister of God's Word, Paul encouraged him to meditate on these things he had been instructed in. Meditation is important in learning and spiritual growth. What are your first thoughts on the idea of meditation and how it can be used for you today as you seek to grow spiritually?

Day 2 – Hebrews 13:15 & Psalm 34:1
Both of these scriptures want you to continually offer thanks and praise to God. This, along with other ideas, was mentioned as forms of meditating on God's Word. What are some ideas you have to stay connected to the Father?

Day 3 – Job 22:21-22
As Eliphaz is talking to Job after his loss of everything, he tells him to be at peace and lay up God's Words in his heart. What verse brings you peace in times of trial?

Day 4 – Proverbs 4:20-22
Solomon is instructing his son to listen to his teachings which were from God. He encourages him to not let the words depart from before him for they are life and health. God's Words bring healing to our lives. Today find a verse that brings life and health to your spirit. Write it and think about its meaning. Focus on it as you pray and as you go about your day.

Day 5 – Psalm 119:16-24
David prays that God will open his eyes so he may see wondrous things from God's law. Read this passage carefully and think

about the different ways David speaks of God's Word. Write a prayer of your own words for God to open your heart to His Word.

Day 6 – James 4:8

The goal of meditating on God's Word is to grow closer to Him every day. James says if we draw closer to God, He will draw closer to us. What would be different in your life if you were closer to God? What would you need to change to make that happen?

Day 7 – Ecclesiastes 12:9-14

Solomon, the wisest man on earth, given wisdom directly from God, pondered on God's Word. He says that much study is wearisome and sometimes we need a change in routine, but that the conclusion of all things is to "fear God and keep His commandments, for this is man's all." As you focus on God's Word today, remember these words. Your all is to respect (fear) God and obey all He has commanded you. How would meditating on His word help you accomplish this?

Deeper Study

Consider the parable of the sower in Mark 4:1-9, 14-20. Each soil type represents a different type of heart that hears the gospel. What would the lives of each heart look like? What actions would be present in each life? Think about your own heart/soil type. How would meditating on God's Word affect it?

Watch for

ABC's

of A Strong Spiritual Life

Volume 2

N-Z

53303929R00131

Made in the USA
Lexington, KY
29 September 2019